LA VIE

A Year in Rural France

www.penguin.co.uk

La Vie

A Year in Rural France

JOHN LEWIS-STEMPEL

doubleday

TRANSWORLD PUBLISHERS
Penguin Random House, One Embassy Gardens,
8 Viaduct Gardens, London sw11 7bw
www.penguin.co.uk

Transworld is part of the Penguin Random House group of companies
whose addresses can be found at global.penguinrandomhouse.com

First published in Great Britain in 2023 by Doubleday
an imprint of Transworld Publishers

A CIP catalogue record for this book
is available from the British Library.

ISBNS 9780857526458 (hb)

Typeset in 11.5/15pt Granjon LT Std by Jouve (UK), Milton Keynes.
Printed and bound in Great Britain by Clays Ltd, Elcograf S.p.A.

The authorized representative in the EEA is Penguin Random House Ireland,
Morrison Chambers, 32 Nassau Street, Dublin D02 YH68.

Penguin Random House is committed to a sustainable
future for our business, our readers and our planet. This book
is made from Forest Stewardship Council® certified paper.

CONTENTS

PREFACE

La Roche is exactly how you picture a small village in south-west France. Roofs of red terracotta tiles, bleached-white walls. Sleepy and shuttered against the blaring sun. A cat picking its way from the *salle des fêtes* to the cemetery. The ringing of a bell from a twelfth-century Romanesque church skipping across miles of rolling, glorious countryside.

My wife Penny and I have lived in this Charente village on and off for three years. Now we live here full time. *Définitif.* And it is all due to a series of accidental seductions; we origin-ally came to France so we could implement Plan A: study organic agriculture (*bio* is a bigger deal in France than the UK) with the idea of taking lessons learned, on lavender and wine, home to our farm in England. Then we became enticed by the way the past is still accessible in France *profonde*; the faded Dubonnet advert on a barn end wall, the baker doing his rounds in his little battered white van with a hundred warm baguettes in the back, Monsieur Lapix's cobbled farmyard, with its ducks and geese picking over the manure heap.

As I write this, high in my study, Madame Roban, headscarf pulled tight against the sun, and as thin as her *vélo*, has just cycled past, plastic buckets dangling from the bars; she is on her way to give her cows a treat, a handful of oats. I have not seen a woman in England wearing a headscarf cycling to feed her cattle since 1984; Madame Roban could be my own grandmother.

Like many inhabitants of La Roche, Madame Roban has a *potager* (a kitchen garden), keeps a few hens, and has a small vineyard; as she says, 'If you make the wine yourself, you know what's in it.' To use a modern phrase, many of our neighbours practise a high degree of self-sufficiency. Indeed, self-sufficiency is alive and well in deep France. Our local Intermarché supermarket, which is four kilometres away in the tiny town of Chefnay, is the size of a Sainsbury's Local. Yet it stocks a full range of chicken, pigeon and rabbit food, plus drinkers and feeders. (The rabbit fodder, I hasten to add, is not for kids' pet bunnies.) In France some 20 per cent of the fresh produce consumed is still raised in the *potager*. So, one day, the Charente sun out in its pomp and its glory, I realized I wanted it: the self-sufficient French lifestyle. And why not? Commercial farming has become a manifestation of the Red Queen Syndrome, where, as with the mad monarch's race with Alice in Lewis Carroll's *Through the Looking-Glass*, 'it takes all the running you can do, to keep in the same place'.

Something else: I wanted once again to live in a landscape where turtle doves purr, and nightingales sing, as they did almost everywhere in the English countryside of my 1970s childhood.

What follows is a year in my life as a peasant in a small corner of France. Living *la vie*.

What could possibly go right?

WINTER

JANUARY

We came off the ferry at Caen at 2 a.m. so a long drive south through the French night followed, the two dogs in the boot of the car. Tiring of the mindlessness of the A10 we took the N route south of Poitiers, through a land dark and deep and very old. The sole light in the villages was from the windows of the *boulangerie*; along the road the plane trees were as regular as railings in the car headlights.

We arrived at the Charente house at about eight that morning in time to throw open the wooden shutters for the dawn, as you do in France. Ours is the last house in the village, or the first house, if you happen to come into La Roche along the forest track. Either way, it is known as 'la maison toute seule', and was the curate's house, built *fin de siècle* by La Roche's priest, Father Jacques, and provided him with a fine outlook over his flock living in the trickle of lanes below. Sometimes our neighbours refer to the house as 'la maison bleue', the latter nomenclature in honour of our particular wooden shutters, as brilliantly azure as the Charente sky.

I think it is the loveliest house I have ever lived in, constructed from honey-coloured limestone (La Roche is situated on a chalk escarpment), and with a frontage of classical lines. The wrought-iron-and-glass canopy, or *marquise*, over the front door, even merits mentions in tourist guides. Last year, our neighbour Monsieur Richard, an eighty-two-year-old truffle farmer, dropped by with a sheet of A4 paper; knowing we were interested in the history of the house, he had found some bits of local records, collated them, stuck them together and then photocopied his collation for us at the *mairie*, the town hall.

Bernard Richard is a shuffling giant of a man, with a Gaulish nose and matching moustache, a swarthy Obelix; it amuses everyone locally that Cléo, the terrier dog he and his wife use to snuffle out the truffles, looks like Dogmatix.

Monsieur Richard is extremely kind, as you will have guessed. He is also deeply sensitive. On the day of his visit, we stood in the front garden, next to the oval four-metre deep *citerne*, which fills from the spring rains on the house roof to slake the thirst of the parched summer land.

'A *curé* with imagination was Father Jacques,' said Bernard in appreciation.

On the way back to his battered white Citroën Berlingo, Bernard gazed up at the legend 'MON PLAISIR', inscribed immaculately on the stone arch above the gate: 'You see, the house was his work and his pleasure.'

Everybody has a fond word to say about Father Jacques, who was the *curé* of La Roche for fifty years, and taught the catechism in the windowed semi-basement of the house to generations of local children. (A single hard oaken pew remains down there in the reverent twilight; the children of the faithful were instructed next to the bread oven – a novel twist on 'the bread of Christ'.) 'Father Jacques was perfectly integrated into the community,' states the official village history. He is buried in the dead centre of the cemetery.

The affection and respect in which the villagers of La Roche hold Father Jacques belies how long he has been dead: a century.

Father Jacques in his black cassock and round hat is long gone, but his good works, of all sorts, remain.

A priest's financial lot being what it was in the late nineteenth century, Father Jacques, with eminent sense, supplemented his stipend by autarky. Attached to the back of the house is a hay barn, which is adjacent to a courtyard containing a square stone dovecot, the bottom of which has two pigsties. Although most of the land has been sold off over the decades, there are still three paddocks, a small walnut and fruit orchard, and the inevitable *potager*. (We also rent a small field down in the village, by the brook that runs through La Roche; three acres in total.) In the *cave* of the house all the kit of *pineau*-manufacture sits about – stone vats, giant wooden screw press, barrel ramp, hundreds of empty 75cl bottles – although unused for five or more cobwebby decades. *Pineau* is a local speciality, a fortified wine drunk as an aperitif. We plan to make our own *pineau*, so one of the first things I do this morning of homecoming, of journey's end, is to walk around the mini-vineyard we have made behind the house. There are eighteen vines here, mostly Sauvignon, and there are twelve more in the walled front garden. (Father Jacques had the long, curving six-feet-high wall absolutely covered in grapes, as the drilled holes for the vines' peg-and-wire support testify in stone. My own peasant ambitions are interrupted aesthetically by my family's flora: plumbago, hydrangea, etc.). But I have thirty vines in total. Which is *pas mal*.

I walk around, coffee in hand, my breath puffy like speech bubbles in cartoons. Up through the lanes of limestone houses, the sound of the church bell comes, calling the still Catholic faithful. Then a robin repeats over and again its winter verse (another form of catechism).

It is the bells, more than anything, that tell me I am no longer in England. In England, church bells dong, rounded and emotive; in France, church bells ting, insistent and intellectual. That and the clatter of shutters, the bark of a yard dog by the *mairie*, and cockerels on four sides.

I am absolutely not complaining. I love France, especially this France *vide*, of wide-open, low-population countryside; beyond our land, there is a hundred-acre field, then a five-thousand-acre forest then, frankly, nothing much until you reach Alsace-Lorraine. There are wild boar in the forest, which is ancient, its borders low stone walls made by many hands, in timeless days. At night the boar leave their forest sanctuary to rootle in the fields, including our three paddocks; and the view to the horizon is the pure, original black of the universe, as Nature intended it. If we go west, we can get to La Rochelle, with its chic harbour-side restaurants and its film festival, in just over an hour. Similarly, it is sixty minutes or so to the pine-fringed beaches of the Côte Sauvage.

But it is cold, this thin, dry air of the Charente; at night you can see the stars so clearly they are within finger-touching distance, and the Pan-pipe wail of the stone curlew carries for wild kilometres.

Feeling the want of a log fire in the sitting room, I go around to the woodshed, packed to its corrugated-iron roof with dried limbs of lime; there are two lime pollards (the large-leaved variety, *Tilia platyphyllos*) in the front garden whose pillar-trunks are sturdy enough to support the sky, but when pruned every five years gift a crop of firewood. The same trees screen the house from the August sun; the linden tree is winter firelight and summer shade.

~

At the top of the track Monsieur Roban the Elder is harrowing a strip of the hundred acres; the land around La Roche is the stoniest I have ever known. (Then again, the nature of the place is betrayed in the name.) The pale rocks hitting up against the harrow's discs make a continuous tin-can rattle. Then a shuddering clang as the harrow hits a boulder; Monsieur Roban stops the tractor, climbs down wearily from the cab and carries a boulder, the size of a lamb, to the grass verge, where he dumps it alongside a hundred others. He sees me, waves energetically, then shrugs at the pile of rocks; I speak schoolboy French only, and Roban's dialect is so strong his words sometimes fall on the stony ground of my understanding. (The regional dialect is more than a matter of pronunciation; linguistically it is part of the pre-French 'Oïl' language group, and has its own vocabulary; the Maison de la Presse – newsagent – in Chefnay, the local town, stocks Hergé's *Adventures of Tintin* translated into Saintongeais.) Monsieur Roban and I get along, however; our family has been warmly welcomed into the village by one and all. We have friends here, as well as neighbours, and it helps that we too are country people, with a menagerie of farmyard animals – horse, donkey, nine hens, one cockerel, five sheep, which have been looked after by Roban's son, Guillaume, for the forty-eight hours we were in Britain settling affairs.

Indeed, in France, they actually like farmers; every President of the Republic wishing to keep office visits the annual Salon International de l'Agriculture outside Paris, and the farmers' dating programme *L'Amour est dans le pré* is one of the most popular shows on TV. The French particularly like peasant farmers; the Confédération Paysanne regularly sees its members elected to regional assemblies. If I ever apologize for our donkey braying – she sounds like a foghorn on max – everyone laughs and says, 'Mais, c'est la campagne!' And if our cockerel gives it full blast at 6 a.m., there are four others in the village doing the same.

At the top of the slope worked by Monsieur Roban the sharp breeze makes crows tumble like black rags in a giant washing machine.

Then from the forest: a wild chorus of dogs barking, car horns tooting. Shots. A boar hunt is in progress; warning signs were already erected as we drove into the village: 'Chasse en cours. Ensemble soyons vigilants.'

Such is the music of the morning in rural France: biblical stones hitting a harrow, the cry of the *chasse*, the song of a robin in a pollarded lime tree, the high notes of bells from a Romanesque, twelfth-century gargoyled church, named for an obscure saint.

After the blue skies, the deluge. In our neck of the Charente, this limitless chalk escarpment with its open fields and hill-ridge woods, it's either a basting by south sun, a lashing by west rain, or a knifing from the north wind in winter.

～

I've spent the morning planning the year's produce in the *potager* (which measures 10m x 10m) and in the rented field. My aim is as modest as it is daunting: by the year's end, I want to supply half our food needs – either directly to the plate or from bartering our vegetables, herbs, fruit, walnuts, wool and eggs. Calculating areas required for the various crops, their growing periods and their harvesting hurts the head, so for a relaxing breath of fresh air I take Rupert, our Border terrier, for a walk in the afternoon in the fading forest. For the third day in a row, the rain is blasting in gunsmoke squalls through the stark trees. Everywhere the oaky, smoky odour of decomposing leaves. Wet moss, curiously resemblant of 1970s green velvet, is the only colour and softness in the winter wood.

The dog, nose vibrating, takes the path less travelled, which plunges off the main track, and is thin, winding and black with the leaf litter of the centuries. He's become obsessed with *sangliers*, wild boar.

Around a far bend: a single roe doe, sheltering in a grove of young oaks that in such weather is no shelter at all. Her head down, body bedraggled.

Unusual to see a solo deer. I suppose she has become separated from the herd due to the *chasse*, which coursed through the forest again yesterday, with its blaring medieval panoply of shouts, sobbing horns and ecstatic bells (around the dogs' necks). In rural France the *chasse*, though declining, is still as much a part of existence as the wind and the sun.

When the doe sights us she hesitates, estimating whether we are likely to breach her safe zone. (Prey animals do not run from predators unless necessary, since flight is energy.) The calculation done in an instant, she runs, swerving, her cotton-ball tail flashing rapidly, like a light bulb switched on and off by a petulant child.

At home, drying off in front of the log fire in the sitting room, I wonder how the doe can survive.

~

Despite my stepmother teaching French, my own ability with the language of Proust became arrested at the teenage hopeful homophonic of 'Femme, vin, Gitanes'. Before we moved to our house in the Charente, we rented a mill in Deux-Sèvres, the department to the north, where I joined my wife – another linguist, and fluent in French – on the nightly sofa watching *Engrenages*, a Paris-set *policier*, on Canal+. My vocabulary of French swearwords became, and remains, fabulous. I can swear like a native. *Putain* this, *chier* that, and *niquer* the other. Thus, when I dropped the milk in the supermarket this morning, absolute hardcore rudeness plopped out of my mouth. ('Pardon my French,' I wanted to say.) More eloquent conversation, such as with our French friends and neighbours, can be somewhat stilted. Not wanting to become one of those expats who lives in a little capsule of England abroad, I am embarking on the Hugo Complete French in Three Months course. Hopefully, my pronunciation will improve as much as my profane vocabulary. Taking my Labrador for a walk around the village early this afternoon, I bumped into Valérie Laval, who lives near the church. I joked about my small-scale farming being like that of Marie Antoinette, and she replied jocularly, 'Le Petit Trianon!', the queen's model farm at Versailles. To continue the conversation, and in the hope she might know a supplier, I said that I wished to buy some geese. In French, geese are *oies*, pronounced 'wah'.

She looked at me quizzically. 'Wah?'

'Oui. Oies.'

'Wah?'

In the end I resorted to sign language, using my arm to wave like a goose's neck, and making hissing sounds. 'Ah, wah!' she said.

On a previous encounter with Valérie I said my children ate like wolves – *les loups*, pronounced 'lay loo'. 'Loop?' Valérie repeated back to me, eyebrows knotting. That conversation ended with me silently impersonating a howling wolf.

I have also, to explain my pronunciation of *lièvre*, hare, waggled my hands about my head like long rabbity ears.

Quite often I recall that in *The Innocents Abroad*, Twain joked that when he spoke French in France, he 'never did succeed in making those idiots understand their own language'.

Last night the *sangliers* came within two hundred yards of our land; going out this morning to feed Zeb, my horse, I see that the border of the Robans' winter wheat field has been snout-ploughed. (The boar work from the stone track, firm and relatively dry; clever animals, wild pigs.) The forester says in bad weather they come right down into the village.

This morning: the pruning of the vines (*tirage des bois*), a practice archaic and arcane. I read the books, and watched the YouTube videos, then I did the sensible thing, and studied the Robans' vineyard. The local method is 'spur pruning' to establish 'a double cordon': a trunk with two outstretched arms. I wield the secateurs with as much delicate savagery as I can manage; a tender cruelty that is kind to this summer fruiting plant. Thus, I strip out yards of old tendrils. Painstakingly. Good pruning is a sympathetic art. I am far from sure that, as far as vines are concerned, I have it.

The sky and the land are gripped by winter's cold. The air has the tang of brass. But there is colour in the landscape painting of *A View of La Roche, Across the Valley to the Wood on the Hills*. Pink berries on the spindle trees on the track, a flock of goldfinches overhead.

And the sky is impossibly blue.

~

Odd, the things one can buy at a garden centre in France; our nine hens (Huguette, Dulcie, Zante, Little Red Hen, Edith, Mistinguette, Marianne, Brigitte, Claudette), an allsorts mix of Light Sussex, Grise Cendré, Marans Noire and Rousse, were purchased from Gamm Vert in Niort, at twelve euros each, and are currently laying an egg a day each. Little Red Hen sometimes manages two. After omelettes, galettes, eggs fried, eggs scrambled, egg mayonnaise, *crêpes*, *flan pâtissier*, *grosses tomates cuites aux oeufs* (the latter following the recipe from Jean-François Mallet's *Simplissime*, over a million copies sold, and the French person's cheat cookbook), I have resorted to pickling the surplus eggs. Indeed, I have become, though I say it myself, a dab hand at posh pickled eggs, using a variety of vinegars – red wine, cider, balsamic – and adding herbs from the *potager* to the mix. So far, I have pickled eggs with rosemary, thyme, *sarriette* (savory), *estragon* (tarragon) and *verveine* (verbena), though only thyme and *sarriette* truly taste good. The jars for the eggs are very low cost, very local; down in the *cave* is a trove of vintage Le Parfait, Duralex and BVG preserving jars. The wooden shelf on which they sit is lined with pages from *Le Figaro*, dated 30 September 1938, hailing the Munich Agreement. 'La Paix est sauvée', reads the headline. The Jacques family were not entirely convinced, one feels, by the appeasing of Hitler; pinned to the wall behind the shelves is a browning, rust-marked notice from the Préfecture de Police, 1938: 'Prescription relative à la distribution, la conservation, l'entretien, la représentation et le port des masques distribués à la population civile.' Instructions on wearing a gas mask in the event of war.

Almost dusk. On the side of the track, putting together a wooden hen house from French maker 'Animal Valley', which has just been deposited by a Geodis delivery guy with commendable patience; on sat navs our lane is *terre inconnue*. The assembly is the agricultural equivalent of the IKEA flat pack, and my construction efforts are unhelped by a headtorch on the blink, air sharpened by north wind and a *notice d'assemblage* being, obviously, in the language of Proust, Zola and Balzac. Our Marans cockerel, Robespierre, 'the Terror of the Farmyard', has repeatedly attacked Huguette, the Light Sussex, pecking her to within a bloody inch of her life, so we are moving her into alternative accommodation, with a fellow Light Sussex for company. 'Il est raciste,' laughs our neighbour, Joséphine, about Robespierre. She is on her way home from a walk in the woods with her dog. We *bisou*, both cheeks. Every time such a warm encounter occurs, I wonder if a Frenchman relocated to my native Herefordshire would be so welcomed into the bosom of village life. Mind you, we are not from Paris. In rural France, being *parisien* is the one unforgivable sin.

In finding our house, our Geodis delivery guy had an advantage over the English relatives who visited last summer. He understood the recherché nature of house-numbering in France, which dates – like so much of French life – back to Napoleon. We live at number 11 on our *chemin*, or track. There is no 1, 2, 3, 4, 5, 6, 7, 8, 9 or 10. Or indeed, any number after 11. We are *tout seuls*. There is space for houses before and after us. Theoretically.

I'm impatient to get planting for real, not in theory, but the ground alternates between iron and mud; the growing season is long in eastern Charente Maritime with its *climat océanique*, but it does not commence in January. So I satisfy myself by implanting the metal posts and wire for another row of six vines in our mini-vineyard. I once romantically imagined such kit would be purchased from a specialist emporium in the claret capital, Bordeaux; Monsieur Gobinau, the local wine-maker, smiled and directed me to the establishment used by himself: Bricomarché, the French equivalent of Homebase. We are on the northern edge of the great cognac vineyards.

~

Another afternoon. Our muck heap is four feet high, and twenty feet long: the rear end of a stabled horse and donkey produce prodigious amounts of manure. It is well rotted, so I barrow loads of it over to the *potager*, and spread it about with a fork. The scrubby walnut orchard of Madame Giraud, which borders our land, rattles with redwings in the cotoneaster bushes. The steam from the manure rises into the impossibly blue sky.

~

We need a special present for a friend, and Penny has the good idea of buying a truffle from the *marché aux truffes* at Saint-Jean-d'Angély. The online advice suggests one arrives at least fifteen minutes early. Duly, at fifteen minutes to 7 p.m., we enter the foyer of the *salle municipale* (a fabulous white rococo confection of a building), which is already crammed, not just with people, but with tension, everybody looking everybody else up and down. A bell rings, the doors open, the rope across the threshold lifts and we are borne along by the thrusting, elbowing charge of people into the galleried hall, which has tables covered in red gingham down three sides, the vendors sitting behind electronic scales, their truffles in shallow baskets; and, immediately, people crouched, sharp-eyed, sharp-nosed before the baskets.

We buy two truffles from the first, most honest-looking vendor we see. Cost? Thirty-five euros. We are cheapskates, dilettantes; some of the truffle lots go for a thousand euros, the haul taken away in metal briefcases by bodyguards to restaurants in Paris. The market is over in minutes, every single truffle sold, the shouting, echoing voices gone, the hall a bewildered void.

None of it was I expecting. The frenzy, or the professionalism of seller and purchaser alike. Over a mushroom.

Interesting, we think, driving home. Could we grow truffles?

~

Late evening. Stacking a *stère* of wood (a very French measurement, invented in 1795 as a metric analogue to the Anglo-Saxon cord, but essentially a cubic metre) freshly dropped from the front loader of Monsieur Burnet's Manitou telehandler. 'Un peu froid,' he had winked at me, getting down from the cab.

Un peu. He was swaddled like the Michelin man in two Agri Ouest gilets, and had a heated cab.

Lined against the white band of the horizon, the trees of the paddock hedge form an ID parade of skeletons; the temperature is still dropping by the minute, but the virtue of wood is that it warms one in the stacking, as well as in the burning. When I finally finish, the moonlight lies in shards in the puddles of the track. In the cracked mirrors there is the image of two stone curlews flying overhead.

We don't have central heating, and a curate's house is as draughty as legend has it. These winter evenings consist of subtle jockeying for the best position in front of the fire, always won by Rupert, and my young black Labrador, Plum, bought a year ago from a breeder near Matha. I first saw her picture on the internet, fell in love with her, fell into despair when I was informed another customer had first pick of the litter. They chose her sister, and I got the dog of my heart. In La Belle France, however, there are rules and regulations for everything, including the name of one's dog; it was the year of 'P', meaning every registered pedigree dog required a name beginning with that letter, hence Plum. (When we laughed with our French friends about this dirigisme regarding canine nomenclature they looked at us uncomprehendingly. 'Well, of course, it is the year of "P".') France is not a country across the Channel, it is a world apart. Along with the rules on dog names came a host of paperwork, including an ID card. For the dog. The Belgians sarkily call the French love of paperwork 'l'exotisme administratif à la française'. They have a point; paperwork in France is omnipresent. Last year, when we booked the dogs into a kennel for two nights, we had to present their pet passports, their medical histories, then initial a five-page contract confirming we had read and agreed the canine *pension*'s terms. 'Lu et approuvé', three small words, but a large presence in French life. When we bought the house, we *lu*-ed and *approuvé*-ed one hundred pages of contract. Of course, no one ever reads the contract. Which is also very French.

Kafkaesque would similarly be an appropriate descriptor for French administration. We needed a French mobile phone, and went to La Poste in Chefnay, where the extremely jolly woman behind the counter explained that in order to have a mobile phone, we needed, in addition to a briefcase's worth of ID, an existing landline phone number. We did not have one. *Impasse!* Much shaking of her head followed. In France, there are steps to be followed, rules to be observed. Then broken. What could be done? The woman from the post office leaned over the form and quickly filled the section 'Present telephone number' with a series of numerals. Our registered landline telephone number is that of La Poste branch at Chefnay. My favourite French rule, however, concerns election polling stations, where there is an official notice forbidding the taking of infants into the voting booth. The notice also informs the reader that, should this illegality occur, there is no punishment.

Of course, if one thinks about it, French numerology encapsulates the national mentality towards rules. These are many, they are to be followed . . . up to a point. Thus the French numbering system is perfectly logical and simple until one gets to sixty-nine, when it enters the realm of the bizarre. Seventy is *soixante-dix*, 60 (+) 10. Eighty is *quatre-vingt*, 4 (×) 20. Ninety is *quatre-vingt-dix*, 4 (×) 20 (+) 10. As for ninety-nine, it's *quatre-vingt-dix-neuf*, 4 (×) 20 (+) 19. All this computation may account for the legendary intelligence of the French, and their claim on the Enlightenment (our French friends refer, with blasé propriety, to the entire eighteenth-century discourse on science, politics and philosophy as 'Our Enlightenment'), yet it also explains why international air traffic control is conducted in easy Anglo-Saxon.

End of the month, end of the day, and the very last job, checking Zeb, my horse, who considers himself the equine Houdini. He, and his donkey companion, Snowdrop, are in the right place, the paddock across the track. And so am I. Winter is properly beautiful under the clear skies of the Charente, where you bed down your animals under the ceiling of the stars and the music of the stone curlew.

FEBRUARY

I've become a white van man. Or, I suppose I should say, now we are here in Charente, *un homme fourgonnette blanche.*

We needed some farm transport. Lately, the skies have been the sheen and the colour of boiled fish eye and the polished-for-sale Citroën Berlingo on the forecourt of the village garage matched.

So: the van fitted the purchasing mood of the day, and then I drove it around, and found it fitted some more. A little white van is the French peasant's vehicle of choice. Everybody assumes the driver of a creaky ten-year-old Berlingo is local, so I was continually hailed down for a chat. On finding I was *l'Anglais*, the only Englishman in the locality, they then introduced themselves. New acquaintance was made. The Berlingo has been social integration on wheels.

Aside from being a mobile introduction bureau, the van's other job is carrying this, that, the other. Today it was the collection of six Pinot grape sprigs from the nursery up in the Deux-Sèvres department, plus another twelve lavender plants, and a fig tree. All to be planted before spring and the rising of the sap. Which is imminent.

A dandelion in front of the cemetery wall is flowering bravely, and I notice too the emergence of the brookside trees in low ground from winter's waste water, the Deluge which is the start and end of Time. There are white daisies on the front lawn, cleavers (resembling green bedsprings) in the hedge, a fat black fly on the windowsill, the first spirals of skylark, and a delicate brimstone butterfly floating past in a sky scraped seemingly clean of winter's thumbprints. Portents of spring, but only portents. Early mornings are still dominated by the purity of robin song, performed from bare branches, against a cold blue sky, and at night, when I take Plum for a walk in the wood, the chill barking of the fox, and across the vastness of the black landscape the fluting of the stone curlews. In the moonlight, among the columns and poles of the trees, the darkest thing in the universe is my own shadow.

On the dry, sunny afternoon of the fourth, I insert the vines in the mini-vineyard, plant the lavender in the *potager* and add the fig tree to the hedge we are making along the stone track; an established fig tree already resides there. I have already planted two spindle trees (the most beautiful of trees in autumn with their bright pink four-lobed fruit), and blackthorn is seizing its chance in a strip unmolested by the steel blades of the village handyman's brushcutter, by sheep's teeth, chickens' beaks.

Spring comes very early to the Charente, a month, at least, earlier than my familiar Herefordshire. Today, 6 February, at 10 a.m. in the vineyard I raise my face to the warmth, like a sunflower. And there are cowslips and white campion on the verges, the cherry trees are in blossom, and the tractors of the Robans are ploughing 22/7 (nothing stops a two-hour lunch in deep France).

Days of wind. And cherry blossom, which falls like false snow.

Saint Valentine's Day. At about ten in the morning, I open the windows of the study, which have become fogged by the breath of man (me) and two dogs, to hear the scraping-metal call of a chiffchaff in the ornamental cherry trees. He is the first summer migrant to struggle 'home' (because home is where the human heart places the birds). A song thrush, high in the pulpit of the leafless maple, joins in, full throat; but not melodious. Yappy, urgent, repetitive. Message not music. The collared doves are mating in Madame Giraud's orchard, loud, flappy and indecorous. Such are two minutes' worth of the sounds of early spring in the far eastern edge of Charente-Maritime.

∼

My peasant life: I drive the van up to the forest, my Hugo French course playing on the CD player (yes, the van is that old; it also has a cassette deck), and spend an hour scavenging wood, as much dry oak as I can find, throwing it in the back of the van, a collection of timber prosthetics. Driving back down the stone track, I find I've reversed my opinion about French hedges. English ecological orthodoxy on hedges is that thickness is all, and they should be low (not least so that hunting horses can clear them). But the scraggy, straggly height of French hedges makes them useful in a way; among the naked branches, blots of last year's birds' nests.

Bright, blaring tannoys of yellow cowslips announce the route, brilliant white blackthorn blossom is beginning the annual chronology of the hedge. Over a ploughed field a stunting kestrel, and on the awkward bend of the track, where rainwater stays for disconcerting days, the puddles lie like bronze shields from a battle long ago. This limestone soil, when pounded for roads, sets like white concrete.

∼

Yet there are still ice-birds; fieldfares squabble noisily, like shoppers in the sales, in Madame Giraud's walnut orchard next door. When will spring finally break free of winter's grip? The price of Charente's clear skies is frost which alchemizes plant and soil into cast iron. This morning, I tapped the white protective shroud we put over the orange tree in the front garden with a hammer; the dome donged.

Anyway, to work. With a peasant's eye for economy of effort, I have a raised bed next to the muck heap (thus easy to fork manure into), and this year I am building three more. So a morning of pounding the ubiquitous green metal *piquets* from Bricomarché with a sledgehammer; the walls of the beds are composed of tree planks we discovered in the depths of the woodshed, doubtless from a tree cut down on the premises. There is something eternally satisfying about eternal recycling, of making do.

By midday, I am straining, not just because of the sleeves-rolled-up effort of knocking metal pickets into the chalky ground (I sent a photo to a friend who replied, 'That's not a farm, that's a quarry'), but because of the heat of the rising sun. One, then two, then three, then four skylarks climb the sky above the green growing wheat of the Robans', and sing a canopy of music, which reaches over me.

Suddenly, my horse goes mad.

We brought Zeb over in October, conveyed here seven hundred miles by Fred from John Parker International. So smooth was his journey that on arrival our nag was torn between getting out for fresh grass, or continuing chomping away at hay in his travelling deluxe stable. After toying with me, a wink in his brown eye, he came down the ramp, settled down, settled in.

He's here to ride, but also here because he's family.

But today, the sun on high, he goes crazy, crashing through

the strands of the electric fence; he becomes tangled, the voltage frenzying him so he makes shrieking sounds which are unhorse. Freeing himself, he plunges into the undergrowth of the walnut orchard, ploughing a passage through flank-high grass and rosehip scrub.

I follow him, up and down the orchard, beseeching: my beautiful horse, my beautiful horse; my jeans catch on the rosehips, and the denim erupts in tufts of cotton, weirdly and cinematically, like popcorn popping.

Finally, when Zeb is exhausted, in a corner, snot-nosed and so lathered in sweat he sheens alabaster in the sunshine, I get a rope around his neck, a halter on his head.

Almost doubled with the exhaustion of it all, I lead him back to his paddock. As he nears it he rears again – a real-life prancing carousel pony.

His left hoof descends a whisper-centimetre from my head, then he rises again flecked-mouthed, hooves pawing air.

It is now I see the reason for his agitation.

And it is startling. In the middle of the paddock, in the brown bare circle where Zeb rolls on his back to relieve itches, is a fire salamander.

It is hideous: reptilian, black, daubed with orange spots, something from under a stone, or inside a nightmare.

The cold-blooded salamander stands there absorbing the fire-rays of the sun on its emergence from hibernation.

This afternoon, 16 February, at 2.15 p.m. local time winter officially passed into spring. The reptiles came out of hibernation. In England, the official herald of spring is the chiffchaff; in the Charente it is the lizards and salamanders. The French for sunbathing is *faire le lézard*.

Energized by the fierce light, the salamander looked at us

imperiously, as if it had forgotten that humans ruled the Earth and believed its ilk still did. When I went into the scullery to wash my hands, there was fresh lizard poo, white topped like Mount Fuji, on the windowsill. We have three species of lizards in the garden, the most common being the wall lizard, though we occasionally sight the ocellated lizard, and the highly exotic green lizard. Sometimes Herefordshire is a continent away.

On the way to Gamm Vert to stock up the van with lucerne 'nuts' for the horse and donkey, plus a new Light Sussex hen to keep Huguette company, I nip into the Maison de la Presse in Chefnay to pick up a copy of *Sud Ouest*, the regional newspaper. While the owner is patiently sorting out change for the excessive twenty-euro note I have given her, I flick through the new Asterix book, *Astérix et le Griffon* by Jean-Yves Ferri and Didier Conrad, which she has displayed on the counter. 'Pas mal,' she says, 'but not as good as the originals by Goscinny and Uderzo.'

For the British, Asterix is an amusing cartoon character who, with portly pal Obelix, duffs up Caesar's legions in a swirl of head-banging stars ad infinitum. In France, Asterix is a national salvationist icon, sitting somewhere in the pantheon between martyred Jeanne d'Arc and rocker Johnny Hallyday.

The Asterix tales are the creation myth of the Fifth Republic. Its *Iliad*. Its Cowboy and Indian. Its *Epic of Gilgamesh*. Asterix the product was born in 1961, amid a France consumed by Collaborator Syndrome from the Second World War, the imperial military disaster at Dien Bien Phu, and the war in Algeria. Goscinny and Uderzo stripped back French history to the clean beginning, to 'nos ancêtres les Gaulois', with a hero modelled explicitly on Vercingetorix, the real-life anti-Caesar rebel. With a sweep of a brush and the line of a pen, Goscinny and Uderzo rearranged collective memory of the Second

World War to become honour-saving resistance against the Romans (read: Nazi Occupation), whilst simultaneously creating a French national identity as a people forever proud and pugnacious. Indomitable. Two thirds of the population of France have read at least one Asterix book, the figure rising to nine tenths of men. And they have supped deep on the *mythologie* in its pages. In France life has come to imitate cartoon art; the citizens of the Fifth Republic are not the people of Vichy, but the uppity *résistants* of a little village in Lutetia.

By Toutatis! A real magic potion for the tribe.

Something else about the Asterix books: they reflect what the truly great Gaul of the twentieth century, Charles de Gaulle, said about his own people. They are culturally constituted as contumacious. Or, in de Gaulle's words, 'our old Gaulish propensity for division and quarrelling'. In La Belle France, there is always some group of workers, from opera singers to stevedores, *en colère*. The farmers in particular are militant, dumping shit on the autoroute, burning tyres, causing go-slows by driving along at 10kph. French workers when demonstrating are just the *bagarreurs* villagers from Asterix in hi-viz jackets.

Yet something else about the Asterix books: France is the most state-run country in western Europe, a place where La Poste dictates the size of your letterbox, and the government bans work emails outside business hours (mind you, who, apart from the boss, could complain about that?). In the Asterix oeuvre the Roman Empire is a perennial stand-in for the dirigiste French state, which is as much loathed as loved. If Asterix is France's ego, Asterix is also France's literary catharsis.

France is in thrall to Gaullism. Asterix the Gaullism, that is.

~

Although we have flower and fruit beds in the fifty-metre-long front garden, and an area of shorn lawn for sitting about on, it could hardly be categorized as formal. The birds know this. A couple of days ago, a sparrowhawk, oozing hauteur, perched in an ornamental cherry tree, and I recalled Ted Hughes's line about the bird whose manners are 'tearing off heads'. The effervescence of the cherry blossom did nothing to make the moment tender. This morning at 7 a.m., I receive my alarm call from a red-legged partridge puffing, chuffing on top of the stone potting shed. (The sound of the male red-legged partridge is akin to a miniature steam engine.) With a coffee in hand, I go out to greet the day. In one ancient lime tree is the nest of a wood pigeon, a rackety raft of twigs; the wood pigeon hen stares primly over the edge of her nest, à la Miss Jean Brodie. In the other lime tree the collared doves are sitting hard on their eggs.

The limes have the stature of Parthenon pillars, but they are deeply creased in the style of old elephant's skin. Up and down the long fissures in the bark, beetly firebugs scuttle, brilliant and scarlet. Locally, firebugs are *gendarmes*, after the original black-and-red uniform of the French police when they were part of the army.

My peasant life. Last year we shipped over my favourite tractor, my Ferguson TE20, sixty-five years old, and counting. It's small, but tough. A Ferguson goes on, and on. A gallon of diesel will do a day's work. The tractor needed a service, and I was unsure whether to have this done that side of *la Manche* (the Channel), or this. So I went to the village garage in La Roche, and asked the Phillipots, 'Can you service a Ferguson TE20?' Madame Philippot looked over my shoulder at her father's classic tractor collection in three open-topped sheds, and with commendable, and polite, understatement replied, 'Yes, we can do that.'

The Phillipots also added to the Ferguson the natty orange flashing light tractors required in French law.

This morning, I drive the Ferguson (orange light flashing) with a trailer borrowed from the Robans down to the half-acre field by the brook; in the back of the trailer, half a ton of steaming manure.

Standing in the trailer, I fork the muck out with flinging abandon. Very old school. On the way back up the hill, I pass someone driving a Fordson. We nod at each other; the international, minimal country person's greeting. (That, or a single finger raised from the steering wheel.) His Fordson was of even greater vintage than my Ferguson; it was not a toy, it was not a museum piece, it was a working machine. By my calculation the combined ages of our tractors on passing was a hundred and thirty years. Very old school.

~

To describe a *potager* as simply a kitchen garden is to lose some sophistication in translation. The *potager* is, indeed, intended to supply the soup pot, but given its origins in the Renaissance it is ornamental too. Function and style in one entity, which, if you think about it, is very French. Most of the local *potagers* tend to floral formalism, with *soigné* lines of marigolds and tulips adorning the veg. The hundred square metres of the Lewis-Stempel *potager* have something of the English horticultural un-officialism Rupert Brooke celebrated in 'The Old Vicarage, Grantchester'. So within its square limits, indicated by precisely placed limestone boulders, and the exact square or rectangular beds, there are rambly grass paths, and quite a lot of weed patches. I like the wild vibe.

So do the hens. I am rotovating a strip along the top, dry end of the *potager*, and have the hens in with me. They are Nature's pest controllers. The spinning blades of the Pubert *motobineuse* turn up grubs and creepy crawlies; the hens have a meat feast. This is the last week of February, and I sow a long line of radish, more in symbolism than expectation of a loaded table. A statement of intent. The planting season has begun.

But only partially for me; by the afternoon I am trapped indoors with a leaking water heater. I try two local plumbers, neither of them available, which is scarcely a surprise. The topic most likely to get a dinner party conversation going is the elusiveness of *les artisans*. France is a big country, tradespeople are thin on the ground, and gravitate to the grand jobs: when I called Claude the local electrician last week, he was away doing the electrics for one of the cognac houses in Cognac. The plumbers are in Angoulême, one at a hypermarket, one in a factory.

Move to France, and you do your own DIY. Last week I replaced the glass in the skylight in the roof, which, after a hundred years of service, had developed a crack. And so added 'glass repairer' to my CV. But – a form of self-sufficiency.

Sticking my head out of the skylight, which is four floors up, I could see for miles and miles. In France the countryside goes on for ever; in England, the anxiety is that over the hill, there is a motorway, a new town; in deep France, there is just more of the rolling same.

SPRING

MARCH

I conceded defeat at about 10 p.m., the fire nearly dead in the grate, the log bag empty, the dogs looking mournful; so I went out to fetch more wood from the woodshed. In south-west France the March days are warm with spring, but the nights are chill with stars. Night and day are different places.

The woodshed is a rather grand affair, a capacious lean-to of honeyed stone built behind the dovecot by the Jacques family in La Belle Époque. But it is not convenient; it is a walk.

My mood, when finally outside, relented a little at the excitement of frost in the air. Moonlight lit the lane. The fig tree was draped with stars.

At the woodshed I'm not sure who was the more surprised: the two young stags standing in the gloom of the entrance, or me. Our house has been uninhabited/semi-inhabited for a decade, so the deer have had a free-run of its land; the sack of La Fermette pony cubes I had stuck inside the shed that morning must have seemed to the deer a miraculous gift from the cargo-cult deity.

The deer had gorged themselves; cubes were spilled over the ground like gravel. For a split-second, the two deer, vital and wild, were picture-framed against the regimented stack of wood. Then, with one exhale of pale breath, they spirited away for their forest home, up the fields, over the horizon. There are few fences, and few hedges, around here; our land is marked from our closest human neighbours, the Robans, by luminous limestone boulders.

The two stags were unimpeded in their progress. A stone curlew was wailing near by, and the vast landscape filled momentarily with the stereo of hoof-beats and Pan pipes.

The absence of human barriers in the local terrain allows a promenade of bizarre beasts through our land. From the scullery window, we have seen wander past, in no particular order, the aforementioned stone curlew (no looker, with its goggle eyes and swollen, yellow knees), wild boar, viperines, a hare as big as a dog, a sniffing wet-nosed fox, a buzzard poking around for worms (with surprising blackbirdish aplomb), though my favourites remain the four hunters in a grey Citroën estate, their shotguns resting on the windowsills, having mistaken the turn on to the *chemin*. They too were goggle-eyed.

But the steadiest animal-promenading recently has been from frogs. Such is their impatience to join in the mating game they boing along in broad daylight, as soon as the sun's rays have softened the scene. Unlike toads, which head to the ancestral pond, frogs will make do with any convenient still water – such as the ditch on the corner of the lane, as it swings down into the village. The mass breeding location of frogs is determined not by history, but by frogs being drawn by the siren sound of each other's voices.

The frog ditch also has a lean-to roof, constructed from an elderly elder tree, bent over to 45 degrees from the weight of time, and tapestried with bramble, buddleia, ivy and wild clematis.

There the frogs, in their tens, sit on the brink of the ditch and croak whatever the March weather; even on The Night of the Great Log Shortage, they were down there making their

Dalek din. On a mild, cloudy night their cacophony is so fantastic that it maddeningly prevents sleep.

I try not to be churlish, however, about our loud amphibian neighbours. A frog chorus is the sound of Nature alive and hopping.

～

When in France, do as the French do is our family mantra. And you cannot really pass for 'a Frog' unless you have eaten frog. Some 3,000–4,000 tons of *cuisses de grenouilles* (frogs' legs) are consumed annually in France. That is 80 million frogs, or 160 million frogs' legs. Now a symbol of French cuisine, the culinary delight that is the hind quarter of the frog was originally foodstuff for the poor, who ate the amphibian in the eleventh century to avoid the Catholic Church ban on meat during Lent. The frog only became *chic* cuisine in 1908, when the famous French chef of the Carlton Hotel, Auguste Escoffier, amazed the Prince of Wales with a dish called 'Nymphs' Thighs'. Escoffier was said to have been assisted in the kitchen by the Vietnamese Nguyen Tat Thanh, better known as Ho Chi Minh, Vietnamese Communist leader. The frog also got a leg-up from the chef René Clément, who in 1952 moved to the pine-scented spa town of Vittel. A resolute frog-fancier, Clément founded the 'Brotherhood of Frogs' Legs Tasters' and the 'Vittel Frog Festival', which at its height in the 1970s drew fifty thousand visitors every April to the spa town. These days, a good French frog for the plate is hard to find; aside from the poisoning of ponds by intensive agriculture, commercial farming of frogs was banned by France in 1977 to protect the species, and the hunting season reduced to fifteen days a year, with the catch eaten at the pondside. (The dedicated frog-hunter brings a skillet.)

In the spirit of both scientific and cultural enquiry, I tracked down some frozen frogs' legs in the local Inter-marché (€4.50 for a packet of 500g, sourced from Indonesia). There are numerous authentic ways of cooking frog, though the most authentic is Cuisses de Grenouilles à la Provençale – which, essentially, is to sauté the legs with garlic, lemon juice, and sprinkle with parsley. I've tried frog legs once before, very timidly, the experience not made happy by the amphibian appendages' fleshy resemblance to miniature human ones.

Mais miracle! Prepared provençale, the legs were, well, *pas mal*. Like chicken, but with the texture of fish.

Cuisses de Grenouilles à la Provençale

Serves 4

1kg frogs' legs (frozen)
600ml milk
600ml water
flour
4 garlic cloves, crushed
1 shallot, finely sliced
20g parsley, finely chopped
2 tbsp butter (Échiré, unsalted)
2 tbsp olive oil
salt and pepper

Put the frozen frogs' legs in a mixture of 50/50 milk and water, and refrigerate for four hours. This tenderizes the legs. Pat the legs dry with kitchen towel, then dust the legs with flour.

Heat the butter and olive oil in a heavy-bottomed frying pan.

Fry the legs on both sides until golden brown (approximately three to four minutes each side). Add the garlic and shallot, and simmer for several minutes. Sprinkle in the parsley. Season. Cook for an additional thirty seconds, turning carefully.

Plate. Serve with a baguette.

France has as many butters as cheeses, more than half of them AOP ('Appellation d'Origine Protégée', meaning that the milk is sourced from the same region in which it is made into butter). The good folk of Normandy will protest that theirs is the best butter but those of us down south find that Échiré melts in our mouths. Like other French butters, Échiré – by law – is 82 per cent butterfat, rather than the 80 per cent of most countries. The commune of Échiré has been making its famous butter since 1894. It is expensive, even when bought locally – Échiré is thirty miles north of La Roche – so the yellow gold tends to be used for grand occasions, and grander dishes, such as Cuisses de Grenouilles à la Provençale.

Curiously, after picking up my Échiré butter from the *épicerie* on the square of Chefnay I spotted, on the drive home, the first brimstone butterfly (*Gonepteryx rhamni*) of the year. A travelling spot of sunshine, and the same hue as butter. Which is why this one fluttery insect gave its name to Lepidoptera in general.

Since France is an hour ahead of GMT, we have dark mornings, and even at 7.15 a.m. there is barely enough light to perform my first farm chores, dinned into me by the years, and generations of ancestors. My current day begins: check equids, check sheep, release and feed chickens. My current privilege is to watch mad March hares box under skies so precisely azure they might be the firmament from Genesis. And the air is filled with skylark song, the chatter of sparrows in the barn, the calling of redstarts in the courtyard, and the timeless wheeling of the village doves. But it is cold, peculiarly and particularly so on our Charente escarpment. Stone cold. There is no ameliorating humidity, no gentling and mellowing mist; ours is a pure cold. This morning there is frost on the west side of the hedge; iced ground, candied leaves. After the chores I walk up the track with the dogs. From the top of the hill: the blackthorn blossom in the landscape resembles puffs of cannon smoke on a Napoleonic battlefield; and the scene goes on for ever. On the way back down the track, a woodpecker is drumming, the hazel leaves are erupting, and narrow-leaved lungwort is resplendent in full purple flower. It is almost an excess of Nature, and then there occurs a phenomenon I have read about but never before encountered. A hare bounds over the stone track straight towards me, and would have ended up in my lap if one of the astounded hounds had not barked at the last minute. Hares do, indeed, have a blind spot to the front.

This morning, however, I have little time for musing on the curiosities of Nature; we are off to a *vide-maison*, the French take on a garage sale, in a nearby village. It's the early bird that gets the worm, it's the early attendee that gets the prize object. As we arrive at the three-storey house, people are already walking away with goods tucked under their arms, beatitude on their visages.

The grandmother has died; the family are moving. The French are different to you and me: they are intensely private; it is quite possible in France to know someone for years and never call them by their Christian name, or enter their house. The shutters on the houses do more than prevent the intrusion of the sun; they create an internal, impenetrable world. This *vide-maison* is not unlike taking the front off a doll's house: everything is exposed; the cassettes of Gilbert Bécaud, lace doilies, *Lucky Luke* graphic novels, Ricard glasses, aluminium saucepans. A perfect encapsulation of French social history of the last fifty years; my era.

Another way the French are different to you and me: they have no embarrassment about selling off the family possessions, which always seems like desperate money-grubbing, or the seeking of charity, the north side of the Channel. In France, the *vide-maison* is merely sensible family commerce, every item presented with dignity just so – the creases on the ironed napkins would have served Jean-Louis Michel, the founder of modern French fencing – and the guides around the house were the kids. Anyway, the French don't do charity. You'll do well to find a charity shop in France, outside the Catholic Emmaus stores. The French do *solidarité*.

My stepmother, who took over the maternal duty when I was very young, was, as mentioned, a French teacher, so I was early inculcated in Francophilia; the *vide-maison* is also a walk through the rooms of my past, in golden sunshine, distant echoes of laughter and the background music of Bécaud singing 'Et maintenant'.

We come away with an antique china sauce boat and a walnut bedside cupboard with a marble top. And woodworm: everything wooden in south-west France comes with woodworm.

The drive home, a mere three kilometres, takes an age, me with the window wound down, tapping the side of the car door impatiently. It is not the amount of traffic – there is hardly any in rural France – it is the type; the car in front of us on the winding road is one of those periodic reminders that France is twenty-two miles from Britain, but a continent apart in culture. The car is a *voiture sans permis*, a VSP. An automobile for which a driving permit is not needed.

Just fourteen years of age? Had your licence withdrawn because of dangerous driving, or a health problem, such as poor eyesight? No problem, you can have a VSP, capacity two people. Certainly, VSPs have a speed restriction, which is 45kph. Enough to kill someone. Enough to clog up the roads by your slow speed. If I was truly French I would tailgate the VSP, headlights on, forcing it off the road. The country people of France, as I have said, are politeness itself. Until they get behind the wheel. Rarely a waved 'thank you' for pulling over on single track roads. The smiling, tinkly-voiced woman from the Maison de la Presse is stony-faced horror behind the wheel of her Citroën C3.

On any long-distance drives – and France is a big country – we always allow an extra half-hour. Again, not because of traffic; with the exception of Paris, Bordeaux and getting off the holiday resort of the Île de Ré, I've not encountered a traffic jam in France this year. On the A20 autoroute, I set cruise control to 130kph on entry, and turn it off on exit. No, one needs the spare half-hour for the phenomenon of the *route barrée*, which is invariably signed one hundred metres before the actual roadworks – which, as the French themselves allow, tend to get done at *escargot* pace – requiring a long retracing of the route. (Truly: in the middle of the Vosges mountains, at 2 a.m., we found the road blocked, with no previous warning on the road. A woman stumbled out from a hut in the trees in the dark, and kindly explained our one and only option: to turn around, and go back thirty kilometres.) The other reason for the 'just in case' half-hour is the peculiarity of French signage, which leads one with admirable clarity to within a tantalizing kilometre of the destination, before expiring. One knows the desired attraction/address/shop is really close. But a sign to its actual door? *Rien*.

～

This morning, I walk through the orchard bit of the front lawn (five dwarf and semi-dwarf fruit trees: pear, plum, cherry and a Reine de Reinette apple planted by us last autumn) and it is flushed with spring flowers: blue speedwell, golden dandelions, and over the dogs' little graveyard under the ornamental cherries a covering of violets, which is a consecration and a reclamation. Life over death. Yet it is the spreading mass of daisies that enraptures. There is an old country adage that 'when you can tread on nine daisies with one boot, spring has come'. There are twelve daisies under each of my wellingtons.

The world is now floriated, colourized. The monochrome days are over.

So are my days of sloth. The ploughmen of yore would sit, bare buttocks on the ground, to determine whether the earth was warm enough for planting, meaning a consistent 6–9°C. The ability to wear a t-shirt at midday comfortably is my indicator. By 22 March, we have enjoyed consecutive days of sunshine and tanning arms. So I have rotovated the brookside field. Up and down for hours, behind the bucking Pubert *motobineuse*. Today I have finished sowing a quarter of a ton of Sirtema potatoes (hardy, and developed in the Netherlands in 1951), but also the entirely more authentic Charlotte, an early potato from the Île de Ré in Charente-Maritime. By hand.

I am almost finished myself, and crawl into bed at nine o'clock without supper.

Three in the morning. I wake bolt upright, Munch's *The Scream* made flesh, from a nightmare about the chickens being decapitated by a scissor-handed poacher. Oh God, I forgot to shut in the chickens last night. I stumble, panicky in pyjamas, wellingtons and headtorch, around to the paddocks at the side of the house. In the two hen houses, all the chickens, crouched and blinking, are safe on their roosts.

Lucky chickens, lucky me.

Alain, who lives five hundred yards away, had chickens taken yesterday night by Renard. Alain breeds black, gamey birds for cockfighting, which is still legal in France, along with bullfighting. As I said, the French are different to you and me.

Yes, you think of bullfighting and you conjure a sequin-flashing, cape-twirling arena in the Spanish city of Pamplona, but south-west France has a bullfighting tradition dating back to the year dot – or 1289, at least. That year, the Running of the Bulls was first recorded at Bayonne, down the coast from Bordeaux. Hemingway, in *Death in the Afternoon*, his classic account of bullfighting, was mighty sniffy about any corrida north of the Pyrenees, writing that: 'Prospective spectators are warned not to take seriously any bullfights held in France.' The irony: currently, bullfighting is dying a slow death in Spain – Catalonia has effectively banned the sport – whereas in France, the corrida is alive and, if not exactly charging ahead, standing on its hooves.

The French fancy for bullfighting is at odds with the country's penal code, which under article 521-1 bans 'cruel acts and serious ill-treatment towards animals'. But this is a nation where *patrimoine*, heritage, is the ace of trumps. Thus, the penal code allows exceptions for bullfights – as it does for cockfights – where there is 'uninterrupted local tradition'. As you would expect, bullfighting is a red rag to animal rights activists. The Society for the Protection of Animals (SPA) has filed cases in cities where bullfighting is popular, including Bayonne – so far without success. Each and every time, 'uninterrupted local tradition' beats the cruelty-to-animals argument.

For the south of France, with its self-conscious *esprit du sud*, the bullfight represents resistance to Parisian centralism. The south likes to lock horns with the court. Ask the Cathars. Now, in southern France, from the Camargue westwards, *tauromachie* is part of the fabric of life. You can sit in a café and hear people discussing bovine bloodlines back to the Ark. Much as *The Times* might publish details of horse racing, *Sud Ouest* (250,000 copies sold daily) publishes details of the bullfights across southern France and northern Spain. Only the other day a whole, star-struck page was given over to a memoir of Manolete, the legendary bullfighter killed at Linares in 1947.

Any iota of sympathy I personally had for the corrida began to fade when I first saw a pike stuck into a bull's back; the more the bull leaked blood, the more my desire to watch the 'spectacle' bled out. All the learned discourses about the bravura of the bulls, the grace of the matador, the art of the cape, were rendered to rubbish as the bloodied body of the bull was dragged from the arena. In 'La Corrida', the famous anti-bullfight song written by the French balladeer Francis Cabrel, the bull asks, 'Est-ce que ce monde est sérieux?' Is this world serious?

~

The chiffchaff, after its long-haul flight from Africa, is settled in its lime tree in the garden; in the cracks of the lime, firebugs run up and down; in the evening, a shuffling line of toads, cult-eyed, undertaking their annual pilgrimage to the ancestral spawning pond down in the village. Daubenton's bats, released from the cryogenic state that is hibernation, hunt the gnatty brookside at the bottom of the village. The walnut trees in the orchard are snow-puffed with blossom, and thick with the promise of a bountiful nut harvest in autumn.

The proofs of spring can be seen around the farmyard, as well as out in Nature. In the barn, the heart of the haystack has been eaten out by winter feeding; and Huguette is broodily sitting on a clutch of five eggs. (Huguette having now been joined by another Light Sussex, Simone.)

There are traditional dates for the arrival of the cuckoo across Europe; in south-west France it is 21 March ... By 23 March I am fretting. There is no such thing as spring without cuckoos. They carry spring on their backs.

My mind is diverted from the absence of cuckoos by the presence of Le Printemps des Poètes, a national cultural initiative to promote poetry. Our active little village is participating and I have been outed as a writer (I was required to declare my professions in the meeting with the notary when we signed for the house, also attended by the vendor, Father Jacques's great-niece). Consequently, there is an incontestable expectation of my putting quill to parchment. I am not a poet; at the mere mention of the medium I come over all purple, and adopt the affected nature-writing style of William Boot in Evelyn Waugh's satirical *Scoop*. ('Feather-footed through the plashy fen passes the questing vole.') So, in the intimate, paved court-yard of our friends Jean-Luc and Marie-Christine, amid oleander bushes, I perform, before an audience of twenty, my first and last poem:

The Ugly Hare (Le lièvre laid)

There you squat like a dun clod of earth,
Surely no mother gave you birth,
Rather you were assembled, dear Hare
From the bits God had spare . . .

And on it went, the dreadful doggerel.
So, now you know why I avoid writing poetry.

~

Penny and I are both on the committee of the village Foyer Rural, another national institution, this one founded to boost social activity in the countryside. A third of the agenda this evening is taken up with finding dates for dos which do not conflict with activities arranged by a neighbouring (and rival-rous) village, a third debating the best caterer for the dos and, the agenda done, the last third: *le pot de l'amitié*, the cup of friendship – an extremely civilized half-hour or so of chat and drink, with nibbles which always include, oddly, to Anglo eyes at least, Haribo sweets, plus galette, a disc of biscuit-cum-cake, which is a Charentais speciality, made by Claudine, 'la reine de la cuisine'. (Cake and wine occupy a significant amount of the Foyer Rural's outgoings.) Dominating the chat is a learned thread on the best local goat's cheese. Someone asks us about the cheeses of Britain, at which everyone else, most of whose families have been here as long as the limestone, hoot, 'Ched-dar!' Mind you, after Cheddar, Double Gloucester, Wensleydale,

I am struggling to name another British cheese. Equally, I am struggling to explain to myself why the British do not produce significant sheep's or goat's cheese.

Afterwards, Penny and I walk back up the hill to our house, under the star-blasted Charente night sky, chatting to Bernard Richard, who lives just below us, in an immense, peeling-shuttered *maison de maître*. Bernard is one of the two village elders, and takes his responsibility seriously. Despite the hour – it was closer to eleven than ten – he asked us in.

To be invited inside anyone's house in France is an honour. There are residents of La Roche, their family having lived here since the Flood, who have never crossed Bernard's doorway.

His diminutive wife, Antoinette, as sparkling as champagne, was utterly unfazed by the late-night guests, and fetched a tray of drinks: Heineken beer, *pineau*, orange juice, mineral water. (Always, the bottled mineral water.)

It is easy to romanticize France *profonde*, but sitting at a kitchen table covered in floral-pattern oilskin, the scene lit by a single, dangling electric bulb, with octogenarian farmers, it is difficult to deny the appeal. The Richards told us, in particular, about their *truffière,* their orchard with its thousand oak trees, the trees' roots shrouded and seething with the mycorrhizal fungi that fruit as the iconic Périgord black truffle, *Tuber melanosporum* – the 'black diamond' of gastronomy, and worth its weight in gold.

Hopefully. As in all types of horticulture, you can miss as well as hit, and truffles are a long-term investment. The Richards are not currently driving a Porsche Carrera, but another white Citroën Berlingo. But maybe next year, or the year after, they will have the truffle crop of dreams. In the meantime they have a savvy supplement to the state pension.

I asked Antoinette, 'What's better for sniffing out the truffles, a dog or a pig?' She looked at me, and laughed: 'It's difficult to get a pig in the back of the car.'

Our interest in their truffles was neither polite nor avaricious, but genuine. Our interest is, *faute de mieux*, mushrooming.

~

My trip in the van to Gamm Vert in Niort last month has turned out to be expensive. This afternoon there was a jolly toot on the track, and I opened the gate to Madame Lapix, the postwoman, in her yellow van. She wound down the window, passed me a jiffy bag containing a book (expected), then with a wry smile handed me a long white envelope with République Française on the front (unexpected). 'Tut, tut, tut,' she said, waggling her head. 'Encore!'

In twenty years of driving in Britain, I never once received a speeding ticket. In France I have received four, and counting. It is not purely the long, straight Roman roads encouraging me to put my foot down, or that French drivers like to hurry one along by tailgating, it is the fact there is no national speed limit. In our Charente department, the speed limit is 80kph; in Deux-Sèvres to the north, it is 90kph. And sometimes on the back roads, one is uncertain as to which department one is in.

At my present rate of receiving 'Avis de Contravention' I shall be banned from driving a normal car, and put behind the wheel of a *voiture sans permis*.

The signs of the Charente spring continue in a rush, like a list read rapidly: rabbity-nosed velvet of ash buds, titlarks bleating 'zee zee' in cherry trees in the garden, the jackdaws' chasing games, blackbirds laying their bluey-green eggs (real Easter eggs), the vines in leaf, in the trackside hedge still bare and ruined by winter. Through the March wood, a cold blast comes on the twenty-seventh, a last grasp of winter's cattish clees; in its bitterness it stimulates the sloe tree into white blossom.

The last day of March. It is raining, though the rain – which our neighbour Guillaume Roban refers to, wink in eye, when I meet him on the track as 'le temps anglais' – fails to dampen down the skylarks. At 7.30 p.m., as I am shutting in the chickens, the forest up the hill booms with 'cu-cu'. The cuckoo has come and all is right with my Charente world.

APRIL

1 April, and I feel appropriately foolish.

Over the years, I've laboured seamlessly through broken ribs (after failing to leap the bull gate with one bound), through smashed fingers (headbutted by a Jacob ram), through crushed toes (thank you, Margot, our prize-winning Red Poll heifer) but now I have torn the ligaments in my knee slipping on the front step.

I have a knee of clay.

Can I press down the brake pedal on the tractor? No.

Dig? No.

Carry a sack on the shoulders? No.

I ease myself into the passenger seat of the car, so Penny can drive me to my doctor, the wonderfully named Docteur Bon-homme. (A case of nominative determinism matched only by a police firearms officer I once encountered called Gunton.) The windows of the car are down, and as we drive away there is the sonic booming of a hoopoe, the clown bird. Before I came to France I had never seen a hoopoe.

At the Chefnay surgery, the good *docteur*, today wearing a Boss polo shirt instead of his usual Polo Ralph Lauren, feels my knee, then goes, 'Pfff,' with a relaxed it-is-one-of-those-things-in-life shrug. (Given that the French shrug habitually, a physical grammar, it always strikes me as curious that there is no single word in French for 'shrug'.) Docteur Bonhomme's prescription is exercise. 'Bougez . . . mais pas de travail manuel.' Move, but no work. Too much stress on the knee.

I was not surprised by this prescription. Pretty much every ad break on French TV comes with a public service announcement proclaiming the necessity for exercise no matter the malady, followed by another infomercial warning of the dangers of snacking between meals. Small wonder the French are thinner than us.

I suffer non-working badly. So I expected to be angry in my hobbling-about convalescence. But I've rarely been happier: I have discovered the gossipy joys of watching village life.

I do not mean the affairs of humans – though they have their interests – but the goings-on of the animals: the village life of the animals, among and in man's buildings and by-ways.

For such noseyness we have the ideal vantage point: the entire village lies below us.

They have their definite rhythms and rituals, the other villagers, the neighbours of fur and feather. The robin starts its day – well before the church bells at 7 a.m. – with a thought-of-the-day refrain announced from the pollarded garden lime. The robin's notes trickle down the narrow seventeenth-century streets, high-walled like pale gorges, to prompt the four cockerels of the village; they, vibrating testosterone, try to outrival each other in crowing from the roofs of their coops. Heads thrust into the blade of western light, the cocks wake Madame Bourbin's ducks, who busy-body rush into their pen, quacking outrage.

It is the ducks of Madame Bourbin, down by the old *lavoir*, the clothes-washing stones by the stream, which rouse the humans, cause the percussion of shutters opening.

Every morning on throwing open the shutters, an anxiety. Over the last fortnight we have lost about a third of our walnut blossom to frost; what was once wedding-white has turned funeral black.

I cannot afford to lose more walnut blossom; I have plans for our walnuts; to be harvested green and unripe in July for pickling and in October for *vin de noix* (a rural liquor of nuts, sugar, red wine, brandy). I have orders placed.

But no frost today; so my knee and I relax for a coffee on the front step, and wait for Monsieur Roban to putter past in his arrhythmic Fiat tractor.

Every morning, as exact as Geneva clockwork, he is ambushed by an urchin-gang of house sparrows at the corner of the lane. But then he always has something golden and seedy spilling from a sack in the transport box.

Nature is theatre. A single magpie ('one for sorrow'), the villain of the piece, appears in the dogwood of the paddock hedge, bill dripping yellow yolk. Around him flutters, demented, a wren.

Over the red roofs, over the steam of my coffee, come the feral pigeons, to work the fields behind the house. By night, they roost in the miniature *colombier* at the top of the church tower, built to supply the *curé*, in days long gone, with easy meat. Almost every building here has square 'pigeonholes', today squatted by the dove's wilder relatives.

Human stonework has other utilizers. Lizards by the score inhabit the stone walls of the houses.

I like lizards. I find them gently companionable. They do not make me shiver because of their cold blood. By eleven, the wall lizards (*Podarcis muralis*) are on the steps and the window-sills sunning themselves beside me. It is already 20°C. On the sill of the sitting room, a glistening green hatch of common lizards line up, proud mini-mes of their parents, as if waiting for a photograph.

Our mutual sun-basking is disturbed by one lizard baby clambering through the open window into the sitting room, requiring me to hobble in after it, before a terrier grabs it for a snack. For half an hour I, waving a kid's fishing net around, achieve a passable impersonation of Jacques Tati in *Les Vacances de Monsieur Hulot*.

Eventually the lizard is caught; it jettisons its tail; this wiggles obscenely, accusingly, alone, for a full five minutes on the wooden floor. The stumpy lizard is deposited outside.

In the heat of the morning, the drone of the insects rises by degree. Above the cistern on the front lawn hangs a mobile of midges.

Highest in the cloudless sky swirl the swallows, scripting lines of beauty. They have a kingdom of their own.

My horse plods through the paddock, releasing the scent of wild thyme.

White heat. White silence. A French village at lunchtime. Only one dog barks, ours, English and maddened by a stray cat which is sprawled like Cleopatra in the hay of the barn.

In the verge of the lane, oblivious to both the yapping and the gorgeous technicolour pixelation of the wayside wildflowers (white star of Bethlehem, purple orchid, yellow celandine), a rabbit pair mate.

It is only midday, and I have watched villagers matched, hatched and dispatched. I am always imploring people to 'Go outside. See Nature.' Truth to tell, we have quite a lot of wildlife in and on our house. Redstarts live in the eaves above the kitchen, pipistrelle bats orbit by night, and wall lizards bask on the windowsills by day. In the attic there are *lérots*, garden dormice. For four months of the year we are plagued – there is no other adequate word – by mosquitoes. Our local Intermarché has a special stand emblazoned 'Kill Insects!'; I have become a demon with the electric fly swat.

~

I was in the garden yesterday evening, tending a bonfire, its pillar of smoke ascending into a sky of equally ashen colour. The embers of the day were almost out.

Always, this standing sentinel over a fire at dusk makes me think of Neolithic hunters in deerskin warming themselves around the camp blaze; soldiers gathered around campfires on the eve of Agincourt (my family fought in the battle, which I tend to omit mentioning in France); helping my grandparents burn the dead bines in the Herefordshire hopyard; my father, in his cardigan with leather buttons and elbow patches. Ancient things.

Sometimes I gave the burning heap a prod, so that its orange sparks leapt up to join the white sparks of the stars, and flames painted primitive art on the walls. The scent of woodsmoke was intoxicating.

Mostly, though, I leaned on my fork, and listened to the birds. Is it not odd that the sunset chorus receives so little attention? The avian aubade has a dedicated 'International Dawn Chorus Day', but where is the fuss for the birds' evensong?

True, the dusk chorus is less intense, and less structured, than its early morning counterpart, where the bird species join in a pattern so regular you could set your watch by them. Almost. (Usually, robins commence singing seventy-five minutes before dawn, with blackbirds, thrushes, wood pigeons, wrens, warblers following suit in intervals until sunrise, when tits, sparrows and finches add their voices.) The evening performance is looser, jazzier. It, however, has its own virtues and magic, especially in April when the trees are not yet muffled by leaves and the atmosphere is free of summer humidity, so the birdsong stands out clear in the chill air.

Perched on my fork in the gathering gloom, I was serenaded from a balcony in the field maple by a blackcap. On the telephone wire, the silhouette of a blackbird began singing with almost unbearable sadness.

And for a moment there was no other sound but the hiss of smoke, and the duo of birds.

The pealing of the church bell awakened the tawny owl, who *kerwicked*, once, twice, thrice, before materializing soundlessly above the garden wall, a favourite perch, but then registered me – and reversed mid-air in flappy, cartoon fashion.

A robin in the forsythia commenced a rueful refrain. The old, ivy-rambled stone storehouse across the lane reverberated with the rattling, canaryish trill of the wren, that tiny, angular assembly of feathers for whom the epithet 'plucky' naturally comes to mind. A song thrush in the orchard joined the ensemble with chanting in minor key.

By now, the sun was lying bleeding on the horizon, the sky gone from ash-grey to the dead grey of a turned-off TV screen. And my blackbird had been joined by four others close by, and almost numberless others in the quiet, still valley.

From the dark wood on the hill came a bassoony 'cu-coo', loud; an incantation pumped through a Marshall amp.

At 8.33 p.m. precisely the Supreme Conductor cupped her hand, and there was only fire-glow, darkness – and somewhere off in the universal hush the barking of a dog. France, the land of peace and quiet.

~

Dodgy knee and Docteur Bonhomme's prescription about 'no work' notwithstanding, there is rotovating to be done. So with my knee strapped (with no less than two knee braces), and a handful of 500mg paracetamol from the *pharmacie* in Chefnay, I fire up the Pubert tiller, and set to work rotovating sections of the *potager*. Working with the Pubert is precisely similar to working behind a horse, the same tramp over clogging earth, the same struggle to hold the bucking plough. Under the impossibly blue sky, in the wake of tilled chalky earth, and in searing-white agony, I plant lettuce, pumpkin, courgette plugs; sow peas and haricot beans in ruler-straight lines.

April lives up to its English reputation and drenches me at five in the afternoon. But the smell of the rain on the wet soil is intoxicating, and uplifting. The French Académie des Sciences published a paper in 1891, 'Sur l'Odeur Propre de la Terre' ('On the Earth's Own Smell'), the start of the trail which has led to our understanding that this particular perfume derives from plant oils and metabolic by-products of actinobacteria released into wet air. The Australian scientists Isabel Bear and Dick Thomas coined the term 'petrichor' for the scent, constructed from Greek *petra* (πέτρα), 'rock', or *petros* (πέτρος), 'stone', and *īchōr* (ἰχώρ), the fluid that flows in the veins of the gods in Greek mythology.

After the rain, all the birds burst out singing, including the first nightingale of the year, from exactly the same low branch in the field maple across the lane as he announced his return last year. (Nightingales rarely sing at any great height.) This is the fourth of April.

～

For a week my knee (it now has its own personality) and I work in the field by the brook, and the *potager,* and I understand why the French verb for work, *travailler*, comes from the same root as the word for torture. But in peasant farming, one cannot stop work indefinitely, unless actually on the deathbed. Anyway, my knee and I plant lavender, savory, thyme, sage, spinach, *chêne* lettuce, cornichons and lemon balm, plus promising packets of a flower mix of twenty-four species called 'Je protège mon potager, repousse les pucerons'. Flower power to repel aphids? I'll sign up. Every day, my labours are serenaded by a second nightingale over in Madame Giraud's overgrown walnut orchard; despite their name nightingales can be determinedly diurnal; indeed, this nightingale is so persistent in singing morning and afternoon, I determine him to be a 'dayingale'.

~

The ancients early noted the musical melancholia of the nightingale, the nondescript avian, the beige bird. Homer in *The Odyssey* scribed, on some stone tablet, of the 'wailing' of the nightingale in the groves. (Ovid overdid it in *Metamorphoses*, making the nightingale's sorrowful song into a tortured tale of rape and revenge.) If Keats's 'Ode to a Nightingale' is the classic British poem about the nightsinger (and, equally, a metaphor for the megrims), France has the equally mordant 'The Nightingale' ('Le Rossignol') by Paul Verlaine:

> *Like a clamorous flock of startled birds,*
> *All my memories swoop upon me,*
> *Swoop among the yellow foliage*
> *Of my heart, watching its bent alder-trunk*
> *In the purple foil of the waters of Regret*
> *That flow nearby in melancholy wise;*
> *They swoop, and then the horrid clamour,*

That a moist breeze calms as it rises,
Dies gradually in the tree – until
At the end of a moment nothing more is heard,
Nothing but the voice hymning the Absent One,
Nothing but the voice – the languishing voice –
Of the bird that was my Earliest Love,
Singing still as on that earliest day;
And in the sad magnificence of a moon
That rises with pale solemnity, a
Summer night, heavy and melancholy,
Full of silence and obscurity,
Lulls in the sky that a soft wind caresses
The quivering tree and the weeping bird.

Sometimes at night I too find dolour in the nightingale's tones, such as when I am alone in the house (my version of a nightingale's bowl-like nest of herbage), my wife away, my fledglings flown. Even the scientists, with their dry-as-dust classification of the nightingale into the oscine suborder of the passerine order, accept the sorrow arising from the bird's syrinx as being defining; its scientific tag is *Luscinia megarhynchos*, from Latin *luctus*, lamentation.

Poor nightingales, there is so much more to them than purveyor of sad songs, the prop of mopey poets, and the patron bird-saint of the sleepless. Instead of the all-encompassing glooming, could we not consider instead the beauty in the nightingale's voice, an aesthetic ideal to which our human music can only aspire? I've been to national operas, and I've listened to Gregorian chants in Gothic cathedrals, but the greatest musical performance I ever heard is taking place outside my bedroom tonight. It is mild and dry, which is how nightingales like it, my family are home (which is how I like it), the bedroom windows are open, and there streams in nothing but starlight and the singing of five nightingales, three in the scrubby walnut orchard (since nightingales are ground nesters, the thorns of the rosehip bushes there make ideal fortress material), one in our small orchard, and one in the field maples of the front paddock. They sing the old favourite hymns, passed down the years from nightingale to nightingale, and I in my turn remember, from a book handed down to me, Izaak Walton's note-to-self that the man who hears at midnight the singing of the nightingale 'might well be lifted above earth, and say, Lord, what musick hast Thou provided for the saints in heaven, when Thou affordest bad men such musick on earth!'

There are nights – and days – when I have to pinch myself. I have nightingales as neighbours.

Everyone who is British living in France *profonde* utters, as axiomatic, 'France is like the Britain of our childhood', by which they mean, depending on their certain age, the 1950s or the 1970s or 1990s.

Sometimes rural France is older still. While we were house-hunting and renting the mill in the hedged *bocage* of northern Deux-Sèvres the birdsong was of medieval intensity. Here, in our corner of woods and arable fields in eastern Charente-Maritime, we are at Renaissance level.

I'll take it. Gladly. And add it to the song of my own life.

~

Perhaps it was the enrapturing dayingale song, but I stupidly left the *potager* gate ajar this afternoon, and the two Light Sussex hens have had a field day. Few creatures are better at scratching up earth than *Gallus gallus domesticus*; all the peas and lettuce require replanting. When I go out to greet my stupidity, Huguette is proceeding to the meat course, swallowing a baby snake (probably a western whip), gulping it down like oversize, wriggly black spaghetti. Her three chicks look on, daunted at this lesson in lunching; born a week ago, they are still at the crumb-pecking stage.

The redstarts have sequestered a swallow's old mud nest in the barn (it's not just humans who recycle), and their peculiar rattlesnake calls fill the courtyard, on the walls of which they like to perch and preen. Every day, the nightingales are on three sides of us, there are cuckoos in the wood up the hill, and one down by the brook which runs through La Roche, and there are chiffchaffs, willow warblers, blackbirds, blackcaps, chaffinches everywhere. They make the soundtrack of my day. The very air is made musical.

But no one will ever accuse the hoopoe of being musical. At Intermarché in Chefnay, stocking up on anti-mosquito citrus candles we spot a hoopoe strutting about the car park like a demented priest from Ancient Egypt. 'Hope it's not flying over to us,' says Penny; the bird's metronomic electronic beeping can grate on one's nerves. We arrive home, to see a hoopoe perched on the roof. Beep. Beep. Beep.

That night Tris, our son, opens his bedroom window to throw a bottle of male grooming product in the general direction of the lime tree, where the pygmy owl beeps repetitively for hours on end. Beeping by day, by night. The things in my life I never thought I would have complained about: the sound of hoopoes and owls. Such is my embarrassment of avian audio riches. We should all suffer so.

~

Obviously, one expects a peasant to be a horny-handed son or daughter of toil. Sometimes, however, I really do feel like Marie

Antoinette on her miniature model farm, Le Petit Trianon. Once upon a time I had one hundred and twenty sheep, now I have five. These are Serge, Sacha, Johnny, Max and Mini, all Ouessants, a heritage breed originally from the island of Ouessant in Brittany; black, hardy sheep, adapted to survive poor grazing. To them, the sparse field beneath their hooves matters not, whether blasted by Atlantic wind or Charente sun. So far, so rufty-tufty. However, the Ouessant is also the smallest recognized breed of sheep in the world. When I took the family to Zoodyssée, a park specializing in European wildlife but with a petting farm for kids, and introduced them to the Ouessant, the first chorus was 'Where?' Followed by 'What!' The Ouessant were barely visible behind the low wall of their pen; indeed, Ouessant are only knee-high. A ram is no taller than 49cm at the shoulder. Sometimes, if I need to move our toy-size five I simply pick them up, and pop them over the fence into the next paddock.

Like today. Do I feel diminished by the lack of ovine number, or stature? I do not. Ouessant, dark and Viking, are intelligent, characterful and very sheepy, in the same way that miniature Jack Russells are as dogged as Great Danes. We have our five Ouessants for their highly prized wool, beloved by craftspersons, for knitting, for felting. (Serge, Sacha and Johnny, all named for French balladeers, are castrated males, or 'wethers', which produce the glossiest, finest wool.) One day the five Ouessants will go the way of all livestock flesh. One day. I believe in the old, peasant ways, and will not kill farmyard animals until they have lived a natural lifespan. Also, we bought three of the Ouessants from an admirable shepherdess in south Charente, who breeds her Ouessants as companion animals, as live lawnmowers, and for their wool, and their utility in conservation grazing. (Ouessants eat down scrub and the more rampant grasses, allowing a thousand wildflowers to bloom.) Max the ram and Mini the ewe came from Zoodyssée itself; Ouessants are much sought after in France – as a desperate but, as it transpired, inspired gamble last year I emailed Zoodyssée asking if they had any surplus Ouessants. They gave us Max and Mini in return for a donation; comically, on the day of collection, the van would not start, so we brought Max and Mini home in the boot of the family German hot hatch. Max in particular likes to be petted, and if I fail to tickle his cheeks on encounter he butts me. He might be small, but his head is as hard as concrete, and he boasts a fine pair of spiral horns. His knee-capping technique is utterly professional.

Aside from the two hundred euros the five Ouessants provide from their fleeces each year, they are my four-legged assistants; they have spent the winter on the brookside field eating down the vegetation (saving me ground-clearing work), and manuring it. Win, win.

Anyway, I like them. I talk to them. In French.

~

Our little Reinette apple tree on the front lawn is in blossom, and in the late evening I go out to inspect it; one has an almost parental feeling towards any trees one has planted on one's own patch. I am just in time to catch a shower. Taking refuge in the door of the stone summer house (a mirror match for the stone potting shed exactly level with it), I watch the rain fall on the floral kaleidoscope of the lawn, and drip on the periwinkle under the wall. Beside me on the doorway, protected by an arch of a lime tree, firebugs mate (firebug mating can take a week) and a swallowtail butterfly, a snip of canvas, blatters about high in the tree, among the emergent leaves; swallowtails are strong flyers. A blackbird somewhere in the ash trees of our paddock across the track tunes up (rather off-key: blackbirds sound either sublime or like Punch and Judy). The grapes are in full leaf; indeed, they are rambling mad, their tendrils growing by two inches a day. In the door of the summer house I just watch the rain, enjoying doing nothing but watching, listening and inhaling a French country garden.

~

A problem with farming is not just the planting anew, but maintaining the old; one of the paddocks got badly 'poached' (meaning the grass was turned to mud) by the equids last winter, so needs to be reseeded, restored; so another hop-along day behind the Pubert *motobineuse*. The grass element of the restoration is easy – the local Gamm Vert garden centre sells a farmyard mix of seeds, suitable for horses, chickens, sheep and geese, as fodder and as flooring, having 5/5 'résistance au piétinement'. I wish to add wildflowers to the mix; our paddocks are species rich. (Pretty wildflowers, perversely, like insipid ground, such as our limestone escarpment.) Aesthetics, a feeling for Nature, are among my motives. Another is practical, hard-headed, and to be put on the plus side of the financial balance sheet. Botanical diversity in the sward is good for the health of the stock. As the old farming law has it, 'Livestock make meadows, meadows make livestock.'

So to the grass mix I add local chalkland staples: poppies, wild carrot, scabious, ox-eye daisy, clary and *bleuets* (cornflowers), the French flower of remembrance. Some of these are 'plugs', requiring me to lie face down in the dirt, make a hole with a crowbar, and insert. In peasant farming, you truly cannot go to your sick bed unless you are dying.

The bare soil is warm with spring. A fritillary butterfly flits by on the balmy 9 p.m. air, and adds tone to the proceedings.

My contemplation of the scene is prolonged; my knee is so painful I cannot stand, and have to crawl to the fence, to hoist myself upright. On the other side, Zeb regards me with amusement, a straggle of chicory hanging from his mouth. Flower power for horses.

The evening sun is low and brilliant red; bush crickets are singing; by the *mairie*, a dog barks; behind the wood on the hill, a single Mobylette moped buzzes. France.

~

We are in the dining room, Penny next to the window, trying to get reception on her iPhone. A bump. A hoopoe crashes into the window, and stands on the window ledge with a startled expression, though perhaps not as startled as Penny's. With their elaborate feathered crowns and sharp decurved bills, hoopoes truly are the weirdest-looking of avians, and it is easy to see how the bird became mythologized, negatively, by the Ancient Greeks. Ovid's *Metamorphoses* is replete with gruesome tales, but the most gruesome is King Tereus' rape of his wife's sister (Philomela), and the cutting out of her tongue. Muted, the sister weaves a tapestry depicting the violation; in sisterly revenge the queen cuts off her son's head and feeds his body to Tereus in a stew. Tereus chases after the sisters with a sword, intending to kill them both. To enable their escape the gods turn them into birds, the nightingale and the swallow. Tereus too is turned avian. He becomes the hoopoe; the bird's crown symbolizes Tereus' royalty, its beak his cruelty:

Fix'd on his head, the crested plumes appear,
Long is his beak, and sharpen'd like a spear;
Thus arm'd, his looks his inward mind display.

Other cultures spin the hoopoe more positively. In the twelfth-century epic *The Conference of the Birds*, the hoopoe is the wisest bird of all. Both the Qur'an and Jewish folklore associate the hoopoe with King Solomon, the wisest of all kings. A flock of hoopoes saves Solomon's life by spreading their wings over him in an enormous canopy, protecting him from the burning sun.

Still, the tropes and archetypes of western culture lurk and linger. I see a hoopoe, and I see Tereus.

~

The last day of April, again blue skies and shorts. The swallows have gone high, a sign of the times, of increasing temperature. I plant another fig tree, close to one on the track where we are growing/letting grow a hedge, then plant up the raised beds with peppers, courgettes and cherry tomatoes.

In the evening, a walk down to the brook with Penny, and the dogs. Pyramidal orchids pronging up throughout the verges. From a poplar, a golden oriole calls out its tropical *we-lo*. Penny whistles to the bird. Who whistles back.

All feeling things express biological rhythm, but the avian circadian clock is particularly complex, the mechanism being an intricate relationship between the bird's retinae, the pineal gland and the suprachiasmatic nuclei in the brain. One can still use the birds as a clock. I am up with the lark, and go to bed with the nightingale. In France.

MAY

From the village clustered at the bottom of the hill: the sound of shuttered silence. Overhead, a single jet scrapes a white line on the blueboard of the sky, and then is gone. Likewise, the ethereal hen harrier, who patrols the vast spring-green wheat field of the Robans. Already the wheat is clotting red with poppies.

Around me on the wide-open escarpment: merely the murmur of bees, the soft lapping flight of butterflies, the absent-minded cooing of chickens, the rhythmic chink of my *serfouette* on the blaring white earth as I weed the lavender. The *serfouette* is a French draw hoe, with a square blade one side, an arrowhead blade the other, wielded like a pickaxe. (The *serfouette* is medieval in origin, but hoes in general are ancient; in the creation mythology of Sumer the godhead Enlil invented the hoe.) The *serfouette* is niftily brilliant at decapitating *mauvaises herbes*. Generally, I have a liberal attitude to 'weeds', so am solely eviscerating the docks and other unwanted plants growing up and through the lavender bushes; the pathways are left to flower wildly.

Georgette Roban is on her way home for lunch, and is on time. The spume of chalk dust from her bike wheels is still hanging in the air as the church bells ting out twelve o'clock, with an admonitory urgency foreign to the torpidity of the day. But I cannot acclimatize myself to eating at midday; or indeed grant two hours to the meal. Or, not yet. Accordingly, I continue my weeding of the lavender; the mad Englishman in a Nike baseball cap borrowed from his son, shirt collar raised to prevent him from becoming a redneck.

A Marans hen follows the hoe so closely it might be drawn along on a string, like the wooden, wheeled toy you had when you were young. There is no child-friendly sentiment, however, in the eye of the real chicken, only raptorial focus; of all the birds, the chicken most closely resembles in demeanour its dinosaur ancestor.

I have two rows of lavender, sixty bushes in total, comprising English or true lavender (*Lavandula angustifolia*), and French lavender (*Lavandula dentata*), two species of the same plant, but with differences in perfume, flower shape, longevity. Curiously, French lavender is not that commonly cultivated in France; it's English lavender that fills the hills around Grasse in southern France and became a key component of perfume. What is in a name? If it is 'lavender', then utter etymological confusion. The English 'lavender' may be derived, via the Old French *lavandre*, from the Latin *livere*, 'bluish'. Then again, its lexical root may be the Latin *lavare*, 'to wash', since the plant was used in bygone days to scent washed fabric.

It scents unwashed fabric too. My jeans constantly brush the lavender bushes, releasing their heady perfume. I smell good (an unusual state of affairs, frankly, for a farmer mid-job). No artificial fabric refreshers necessary.

I confess, *j'aime la lavande* as well as the *serfouette*.

There are many reasons for my love of lavender, and one is the herb's immunity to birds and beasts. No wandering Marans fowl, wild deer, promiscuous rabbit from the overgrown walnut orchard, or escaped Limousin cow from the Robans' herd will touch this member of the mint family. I like to think of myself as a farmer-conservationist, a farmer with an 'alter-eco'; sometimes I think I am just a tired one, and that a crop as robust and repellent to avians and fauna as lavender is a godsend.

It is Provence that is famed for its blue lavender landscapes; but we have much the same droughty, stony *terroir* here in western Charente. Stones are good. Stones bounce the sun's rays back on to the lavender. Stones irradiate the lavender in reflected light and stored heat.

I stand for a moment, to stretch my back and rest the knee: everything solid in the landscape beyond a hundred metres has melted into treacly air. The far, rolling and wooded ridges have gone. There is only me, the hens and Nature, stranded on a quarter of an acre of bee-drowsy, perfumed Lavenderland.

Then back to work. The wildflowers that fall to my *serfou-ette* are the thirsty and the tall. So adieu, today at least in Lavenderland, to docks, thistles, lords and ladies, the siren and serpenty field bindweed.

What is left on the earth is chromatic and mosaic: the pretty and the meek little field flowers, in their speedwell blues, pim-pernel reds, chickweed whites, cranesbill pinks.

My hoe strikes a submerged boulder. On the top of the great white lump I see the imprint of a fossil seashell, ghostly and pale. In the Cretaceous period the landscape around me was ocean, another sort of vastness. And it was a time even more remote than now.

~

4 May, and we reach peak nightingale; another male landed yesterday, so now there are six around the house. The late

arrival is cocksure, and loud, and stands proud in the ash, defy-ing the wind coming down the escarpment. I am awed by his stamina, and then I wonder: do trees get weary in the wind, with all the shaking and blowing about? Is their creaking the sound of suffering?

There are other avian arrivals; a pair of turtle doves, in the deep cover of the field maples, now fully leafed, purr away. I am compiling a list of the birds nesting around – and indeed in – the house, plus the garden. So far, there is a blackbird in the forsythia, a collared dove in one lime tree, and wood pigeon in the other, a wren in the *cave*, and swallows in the hay barn.

In the wind and the dust and the nightingale song, I finally get around to trimming the medusa-headed vines, snipping away the excess suckers and leaves – and have the bright idea of using the latter for lunch, by flash-boiling them in salted water, and then wrapping them around blocks of feta and thyme (from the *potager*) to bake in the oven. Penny, who gen-erally dislikes cooked vine leaves, pronounces My Big Fat Greek Lunch 'really excellent'. The lunch, in preparation and consumption, takes a leisurely French hour or more.

Feta Baked in Vine Leaves

Serves 2

12 large fresh vine leaves (or equivalent)
200g block of organic feta
¼ unwaxed lemon, grated
2 garlic cloves, crushed
1 tbsp red pepper, chopped
5 sprigs fresh thyme

5 leaves fresh mint
black pepper
olive oil
sprigs of mint (for decoration)

Boil the vine leaves in salted water for five minutes, strain, and lie flat. Preheat oven to 220°C, and line a small baking tray with aluminium foil. Grease with olive oil.

Lay out a mat of vine leaves (just over half of them), and place the feta block on top.

Spread the lemon, garlic and red pepper over the top of the feta; add the thyme sprigs and the mint leaves, and top with several hard twists of black pepper and a drizzle of olive oil.

Spread the remaining vines over the top, and wrap the block into a neat parcel. Fold the foil around the vine-leaf block, place the tray in the middle of the oven. Bake for twenty-five minutes.

Serve with sprigs of mint for decoration, and a green salad.

In the afternoon, I come over all *The Good Life*, and make 'briquettes' from pulped copies of *Sud Ouest*. (For the sadly uninitiated in briquette-making, one soaks ripped newspaper in water, then pours the pulp into a metal briquette-maker, presses the handle to squeeze out water, and leaves the briquette to dry in the sun.) My metal briquette-maker was a Christmas present.

I do not know if, by some internal weather-awareness, my briquette-making anticipated a change in the weather, but days of cold weather follow. *Sud Ouest* is full of laments from winemakers concerning the frost; the temperatures drop to their lowest locally in fifty years; 15 per cent of the cognac crop is affected. Our vines, thankfully, are sheltered and suffer little ill. The French term these returning wintry blasts in the second week of May 'The Days of the Frost and Ice Saints', or in the words of Rabelais, 'Ces saincts passent pour saincts gresleurs, geleurs, et gateurs du bourgeon.'

Guillaume Roban, passing by on his bike (all the Roban family whizz around on bikes, when they are not in the seat of a tractor), is gloomy about their vineyard, which is fully exposed. Then he sees my electric fence, and protests that I have not taken it right up to the edge of my own land. He goes off to his barn, gets a post, a sledgehammer and a metal borer, bangs in the post, attaches the plastic screw to hold the polywire. 'Right up to the edge of the wheat!' he says. In England I can safely say I have never been asked to maximize my land; there fences consist of fellow farmers looking at them saying, 'I think that's on my land, you need to move it back a bit.' A consequence, I suppose, of living in a more crowded country.

~

The wood is in its White Period. Guelder rose, elder and hawthorn are all in bloom, the latter heavily. Last evening, standing on the grass track alongside the wood was to observe a crashing phosphorescent wave, as if seen end-on. The illusion was completed by the daisies, dandelion clocks, stitchwort and white campion at floor level; a sort of surfy swirl. But no saltwater is as good on the nose as woodland edge in spring, particularly after a light shower has amplified the smells. White campion can match honeysuckle as perfume (ask the moths), and common hawthorn, with its aroma of spicy almonds, is the very stuff of aftershave.

Or I, at least, would label hawthorn thus. Smell – surely the most underrated, under-utilized of our senses when enjoying

Nature – can be particular, and tricky. Others note *Crataegus monogyna*'s animalic nuances. In his *Englishman's Flora* of the 1950s Geoffrey Grigson explained how French boys used to use hawthorn branches as a philtre, putting boughs outside the windows of every young girl in the village. The aphrodisiacal aspect of hawthorn, of course, extended to Medieval England, with its romantic rituals of 'a-maying' and dancing around a 'Maypole', originally a hawthorn tree in flower.

~

Like the wood, the lane is in its White Period, with the floral discs of elder floating like flying saucers in the dusk. Elderflower, whether for cordial or champagne, is best picked in the morning, but the morning has been appropriated by picking and drying the first harvest of herbs (savory, mint, sage, rosemary and bay, which grows wild in our hedges), so I am picking the elderflower this evening. It takes less than half an hour and I have filled five long-life bags from Intermarché (or 'L'Inter', as we locals say), then go into the scullery to make elderflower champagne in giant 8-litre Volvic bottles. On the lane, above even the sweet smell of elder-flower, there was the stink of lizard orchids, whose evolutionary niche is to emit an odour like meat on the turn.

The lizard orchid, *Himantoglossum hircinum*, takes its name from the appearance of the flower due to its grey-and-green coloured bloom and ragged side lobes which give the impres-sion of the legs and tail of a lizard. There is a true reptile in the *potager* the next morning, as opposed to a plant imitation: a dead western whip snake, a metre long, with a lemon-yellow underside and black Fabergé pattern on its top side, lying across a row of potatoes. I am not a lover of snakes, but I acknowledge its strange beauty. Since I can hardly leave it among the potatoes, I lift its stiff S-bend body (quite weighty) gingerly up with a fork, then suffer an agony of indecision as to its disposal, and stand in my very own H. M. Bateman cartoon: 'He did not know what to do with the deceased serpent.' Eventually, I decide on the manure heap, and bury it deep in the bottom. This I feel, in retrospect, is hardly Solomonesque sense; will I want to disinter a snake's corpse when digging out the manure? Ever? A section of the manure heap, I suspect, will for ever be untouched.

My uncomfortably close encounters with snake-kind continue. A day later, entering the *potager*, a whip snake hisses at me, violently, before oozing away into the pile of stones I have erected there as a herparium (I know, I know: I made a space for reptilian nature, so what did I expect?). Over the next three days, the snake encounter recurs, a frame of film repeated, and I realize that the snake is the mate of the deceased, and I, for the first time ever, contemplate whether snakes can have finer feelings. Love in cold blood.

But love in a hot land of little rain. It is only May, but the thermometer on the barn wall is hitting 29°C, and daily I fill the birdbath in the courtyard with water. (The birdbath is a mini stone trough, found under the heaped remains of the stone balustrade which formerly lined the front steps of the house, and which are now piled decoratively in the courtyard as romantic ruins.) Plum plays in the birdbath with her nose, after which it is visited successively by goldfinches, a cirl bunting and a wood pigeon. Sometimes, the easiest conservation aids are the most successful conservation aids.

Late evening, sitting in the walled front garden, watching the sun go down, a glass of elderflower champagne in hand, salade niçoise on the table (using our own eggs, radish and lettuce), bicycles parked against trees, citronella candles flickering – a very French scene, made even more so by the coming of our twin ancient lime trees into leaf. The scientific name of the broad-leaved lime, *Tilia platyphyllos*, notes perfectly the plate-like flat broadness of its leaves. There is the slightest whisper of wind this evening, and the limes take full canvas. We are sailing along. My knee is 50 per cent better.

~

In addition to the woodshed and dovecote the house has, to the rear, a small barn. The great, hidden advantage of being a Nature lover is that one does not feel a pressing need to do buildings up. On the contrary, I am, to a degree, letting the barn, with its stone walls, trunks as roof beams, and corrugated-iron roof, go to shack and ruin. As long as it does the job – keeping hay and farm kit dry – I am supremely relaxed about the aesthetics. The problem with modern buildings is that they rarely, if ever, give Nature a home; on the contrary they are tidy, sterile mausoleums for the wild things that inhabited the space previously. So in our barn, cracks in the brick floor emit 'weeds' such as dandelion, ivy is permitted to grasp the side walls, wild clematis grips the rear wall; an elder tree authorized to stand sentry at the entrance. We have also given Nature a helping, if minimal, hand: a downspout twisted around so rainwater creates a muddy puddle; and, to stop the wind whipping around the rafters, a partial front 'wall' has been fashioned from mildewed straw bales, behind which sparrows feed on spilled grain. It is a place of echoes and shadowed corners.

The naturing of the barn has fruited. The ivy is wren-roosted; sparrows and finches pick at weed seeds in the haven behind the bale wall; a robin nests in a crack between the said bales; swallows use the puddle as their brick factory, and are proving the truth of their full name, 'barn swallows', by gluing their nests to the beams. Pipistrelle bats have a good place to hang upside down in.

One consequence of the naturing of the barn is pleasantly and wholly unexpected; I find it a good place to be, tranquil and soothing. With shafts of high sunlight catching dancing motes of dust, it has something of the atmosphere of a temple in the afternoon. The smells help; under the pervading fresh-laundry scent of hay and straw, are airs of rotted sack, and weathered timber. Inhale deeply, and you inhale the past.

In our small village, population 190, there are at least fifteen houses and barns in a similar state of characterful disrepair. The picture is the same across rural France. Most of these buildings are not intentionally neglected (as is the case with our barn) but are the consequences of depopulation and Napo-leonic inheritance laws, by which children are 'protected heirs' and cannot be disinherited. A family feud between them pre-vents resolution, no division of the property taking place, and a file that can then sit in the pending tray at the office of the local *notaire* for an eternity.

The physical pending tray, that is, rather than the electronic one. France can be so, so modern, as when one is whizzing along at 200kph on the TGV railway from Paris Montparnasse to Poitiers. In our village, thanks to the mast next to the water tower (gloriously, this is the *château d'eau*) on the hill, we have five whole bars on the mobile. But never, ever expect a reply to an email in France. The snail mail of state-owned La Poste, however, always works on time. Like the trains. Also, with a nicely human touch, the post person of La Poste will, on his/her rounds, check on aged relatives.

According to Insee, the French national statistics office, there are over three million empty homes in France, or 8.4 per cent of the total housing stock. In 17 per cent of communes – the basic administrative division in France, the nearest British but less powerful equivalent being the parish or urban district – the rate of vacancy is over 20 per cent. Little of rural France is redeveloped and twee.

~

Yesterday evening, up in the wood a cuckoo was booming its woodwindy diphone call.

According to country law, when a cuckoo sings evensong, fair weather follows the next day. The bird did not deceive. At about eleven this morning I go out to collect the eggs. Above, blue sky and the liquid chatter of swallows. Beneath, plant growth so vigorous it seems to lift you up. Everywhere, the bearable lightness of being. Summer has deigned to visit.

The paddocks are erupting in flowers: ox-eye daisy, daisy, red clover, white clover, poppy, ragwort, docks, plantain, yarrow, clary, white campion, wild rose, field bindweed, pyramidal orchid, burdock, poppy, meadow buttercup, chicory and shepherd's purse, to name but nineteen.

Then the bright day collapses into ruins; as I lift the lid on a nest box on the gig hen house I spot ashy smudges on the wood. Any hope is killed on taking the nest compartment apart; in the joints seething, glistening blobs of red mites. In twenty years of poultry keeping in Britain we evaded the scourge, but France is hot and mite-friendly. The mites literally suck the blood out of hens. I scrub everything, lay it out in the sun, and drive over in the van to the Gamm Vert at Saint-Jean-d'Angély to buy a bottle of Saniterpen's 'Répulsif Insectes', a white talcum-powder-like stuff containing 'pyrèthre végétal'. It is the nearest organic, natural solution to the problem I can find. I don't want to push the nuclear button of inorganic. On the journey there and back, I give the Hugo French course a miss, and listen instead to France Bleu on the radio, a useful mix of magazine chat and music for the wannabe French speaker. I once thought, somewhat xenophobically, that all modern French pop music was sub-Johnny Hallyday fifties-type rock; these days I seem to be an ambassador for *musique et chansons française*. Anyway, on the radio comes the arty-punky Les Rita Mitsouko with Catherine Ringer belting out 'C'est comme ça' from 1986. I've got the window down, elbow out, and am driving along the four-kilometre stretch of minor road from Chefnay to La Roche; I pass two cars coming the other way, one driven by Franck and one by Valérie. Both Franck and Valérie have the car radio pumped up and 'C'est comme ça' blasting out through the open windows. Our friend Coralie once told us how, sitting in a bar in Majorca in the late 1980s, the DJ put on 'C'est comme ça' and, 'All the French went wild and started dancing.'

~

I went nightwalking again last night, took the three dogs up into the vast and silent forest. Not a soul stirred; under the wild moon the wind blew echoey tales of the French Resistance. Eighty years ago the Bois des Chaumes was a base for the Forces Françaises de l'Intérieur, the armed resistance during the Second World War. Far into the wood is a marble memorial to Sergeant Jean Cosset of the FFI, killed by the Germans on 15 August 1944. The term 'Bataille' in France does not always refer to military events of centuries ago.

Last night the moon was gibbous (the illuminated part being greater than a semicircle, less than a circle; we nightwalkers have our own word hoard, traced by our fingers over dictionaries in the owl hours; we lucubrate). The imagination can run rampant on such a night and in such a place, where there is no polluting streetlight glare, and the one pair of car headlights coming down the far hill as I reached home is romantic, and in the mind becomes a Resistance Traction Avant returning from some secret mission.

~

By the same token that our house gave Father Jacques a fine outlook over his flock in the lanes below, I have an eyrie over my neighbours' *potagers*. Every house in the village down the hill has a *potager*, even the two new bungalows. 'Grow your own' is a philosophy and a praxis alive and well in deep France.

Our *potager* is approaching its period of bounty. Since it is the aesthetic of Nature I admire above all others, I do not insist on a conceptual cordon sanitaire between cultivated crops and weeds, which, I think, is rather Francophiliac of me. After all, dandelions are still a staple in French salads. Madame Roban, across the sunflower field, makes a *superbe* sauce from sorrel. So the square limits of the *potager*, while indicated by precisely placed pale limestone boulders, are running with the native flowers of the chalkland escarpment: chicory, scabious, corn-flower, poppy, campion, herb robert, buttercup, ox-eye daisy, wild clary clad with imperial purple flowers, and pyramidal orchids wearing purple beehive hairdos.

Each day, the loose stone wall around the *potager* rises a tad higher; on this stony ground, the most obstructionist rocks need to go somewhere, so on the wall they go. (When I rotovate the patch with the Pubert Meso *motobineuse*, the chink-clank of geology against the steel blades is entirely reminiscent of Stock-hausen's *Kontakte*.)

Above the knee-high stonework and wildflowers, one end of the *potager* is a rustic stone barn, scrambled by ivy. The remaining three walls are walls of sound fabricated from birdsong. So my *potager* has the first prerequisite of this French institution: cloistral calm. It is somewhere to reflect, and relax. Reinflate the spirits.

Inside the four walls, the wildflower theme continues: the five long veg beds are divided from each other – somewhat haphazardly – by narrow 'meadowy' paths. Below the veg beds, framed by borders of sowthistle and hawkweed, wild chicory and scabious, a line of electric blues, imperial purple of clary, are four squares of salad, potato and herbs from dill to verbena via parsley, thyme, hyssop, *estragon*, sage, lavender, *oseille* (botanical sorrel, and slang for money), rosemary, mint, lemon balm, *sarriette* and my new favourite honey sage. Wild marjoram spreads like petrol-aided wildfire, and is underfoot on the pathways, so the tread of wellingtons releases its piquant aroma into the herbal air-mix.

My *potager* is a perfumed garden. It is also a feast for the eyes; in addition to the *flore sauvage*, there are small clumps of cultivated wallflowers, alyssum, nasturtiums, dahlias. Nature deserves a helping hand.

As for vegetables and salad, I grow what Father Jacques grew: cabbage, potatoes, lettuce, spinach, radish, peas, haricot beans, chicory, onions and garlic (of course), not omitting *mâche* or lamb's lettuce, that Gallic salad stalwart, which never really appears on British plates. Oh, and I also grow tomatoes and courgettes, which last year provided such a glut that I understood why the French invented ratatouille.

I know the Good Father's planting regime; tucked away behind a table in the potting shed were remnants of Vilmorin seed packets from around the time of the Great War. Vilmorin is the oldest seed company in the world, founded in Paris in 1743. There are still people who use M. M. Vilmorin-Andrieux's *Les Plantes potagères*, published in 1883, as their self-sufficiency bible. Such as myself. The English-language version appeared in 1885.

To be honest, before I lived in France I thought the concept of *terroir* was a nifty marketing trick by the Gallic Department for the Advancement of Agriculture. Now I am convinced by *terroir*, the notion that a site's geology, latitude, elevation, exposure to sun – Nature's grants and constants – express themselves in the crop grown there. I believe I can taste our *terroir* in everything picked from our plot. Yesterday, I lifted our first potatoes of the year, Sirtema, cooked them with mint – from my all-provisioning *potager*, naturally – and in the mouth, ahh, that salt-hint of health and minerality.

I was brought up to believe that the British are the nation of gardeners, but, traitorously, I think that the French may have the edge these days with their commitment to good food, seasonal food. *Mon potager*: satisfier of stomach. And soul.

But the French devotion to the *potager* is about French identity too. To cut spinach from the *potager* for lunch is to continue in the eternal, rural ways – a sort of French resistance to the mondialization of life, in the same way that L'Académie française contends Anglo-Saxon incursions into the language of the Hexagon. France may be the home of some of the world's leading luxury brands (Louis Vuitton, Chanel and Hermès), and may be a member of the European Union, but it is resolutely nationalistic. In their hearts the French do not consider France part of the EU, but the EU as an extension of France. Free trade in France is a chimera; effectively the country operates a cultural tariff system. Above the meat counter of Leclerc supermarket, the biggest chain in France, hangs a sign: 'All our meat is French.' Pick up *anything* in France, from dog food to pencils, and it will say loud and clear, 'Fabriqué en France' or, occasionally, issue the horror warning, 'Contains non-French ingredients'. Go to a French car park: 60 per cent of the cars will be Peugeot, Renault or Citroën. Where do the French go on holiday? France. On the national holiday of Bastille Day, every French *mairie* and every French memorial is hung with the tricolore, often several times over. On Remembrance Day we stand in the cemetery of La Roche beside the war memorial, where Maire Alice Gaitier – wearing a *tricolore* sash – intones the names of the dead, and we respond, 'Mort pour la France.' Not the apolitical, 'We remember them,' but, 'Died for France.'

All this is fine by me. France is France.

～

Today, I cut lettuce, of which we grow five or so different types, varying in colour, appearance, taste. I may not yet have succumbed to the two-hour lunch, but I daily note the frenchification of dinner, now set at 8 p.m., and the number of courses gone from two to four, including lettuce as a palate cleanser before pudding.

Another frenchification: I have taken to cycling to Chefnay to fetch the morning baguette and a copy of *Sud Ouest*. Sometimes, instead of taking the *route principale* on the way back, I take the network of stone tracks. So I am on the descent from the forest towards La Roche, when I see Franck ahead of me; indeed, Franck is difficult to miss. He works for a road-mending crew, and habitually wears an orange hi-viz vest, on duty and off. Currently he is on holiday, having constructed a *pont* – a French obsession where the personal holiday allowance bridges public holidays and weekends to make a very long break. (There are three French public holidays in May; by using only three days of annual leave Franck has ten days off.) Like everyone in the village over fifty, with the exception of Linda, a teacher, no one speaks any English, but Franck and I have a routine after we have done 'Ça va?' and the *météo*. If I am on the bike I say, 'Le Tour de France l'année prochaine!' and he roars, 'Trop tard!' I must have looked quizzically at the carrier bag he was carrying, for he opened it up, and showed me. It was full of blackthorn leaves and shoots. At which I looked more quizzical still. 'Pour l'épinette,' he explained.

Eventually, I understood: the leaves are for a 'wine of thorns' drunk as an aperitif called *épinette* locally but also known as *épine* and *troussepinette*. I explained that in Britain we make an aperitif – sloe gin – from the blackthorn fruits. He looked dubious. As dubious, I suspect, as I looked at the concept of *épinette*.

That evening, while we are watching the *Journal*, the eight o'clock news, on France 2, we hear loud knocking at the front gate. I open the door, and there is Franck. 'You need a bell!' he says, and hands me a vintage Johnnie Walker bottle. 'Épinette.'

Épinette

Recipes for *épinette* tend to be passed down orally, and vary from house to house, but basically the wine of thorns is a maceration of the blackthorn – or hawthorn – shoots (some devotees insist on adding a handful of twigs) soaked in a sweet wine for at least two weeks, to which brandy is added. The drink has a distinct, pleasing almond flavour. It improves with age.

600g sugar (dissolve in the wine beforehand)
5 litres full-bodied red wine
large handful tender young shoots/leaves of blackthorn
   or hawthorn
1 litre cognac

Dissolve the sugar in the wine. Then add remaining ingredients and mix well. Leave for at least a month, stirring regularly. Filter and bottle.

I really do have no wish to sentimentalize rural France, to picture it as quaint; it has its problems of unemployment, and the inroads of 'progress'; at night the red-eyes of wind turbines blink blood on the western horizon towards La Rochelle, sixty miles away. But rural France does still have a pleasing foot in the past, intentionally so. 'P' in the French alphabet stands for *patrimoine*, meaning heritage; the French are, arguably, as well as patriotic, the most history-minded people in Europe. Anyway, to enter the local *boulangerie* is to step back in time; there is no till, only a drawer with spilling notes; the floral wallpaper must be fifty years old; the glass display cabinet on the Fablon-covered counter is unchilled. The glass-and-wood box exhibiting cereal grains is antique. The ten types of bread on sale are held in wooden racks. Madame, with her hair dyed as black as raven's wing, is eighty-five, her son, sixty. We, the loyal customers, form an orderly queue out into the tree-lined square, and shuffle forward to receive the benediction of their bread. A secular communion. I ask for *baguette à l'ancienne*, which madame shuffles into a paper wrapper. On the way out, I meet my friend and neighbour Jean-François. 'Toujours comme ça,' he says, referring to the length of the queue. The baguette purchased, it is impossible to resist a coffee on the terrace of Le Marché, the *bar-tabac* which overlooks the lime-tree-lined town square.

The rituals of rural France, whether queuing for a baguette or sipping a *noisette* (espresso with a 'nut' of milk) while watching the world go by, are effective barriers to the rush of modern times. Somehow, in France, at least outside Paris and Marseille and Lyon, there is still time. Time to chat. Time to be. Time to do nothing at all.

I watch Jean-François make his way from the *boulangerie* to the Maison de la Presse. A journey of fifty yards, but it takes Jean-François quarter of an hour. A former notary in his early seventies, Jean-François shakes hands or *bisou*s five different men and women – France is the republic of handshakes and kisses – and exchanges greetings, gossip and news with them all. These same people then greet and talk with others in a slow, slow quadrille.

I sit sipping my *noisette* and watch the dance to the music of time.

Cycling home, baguette in one hand, I fail to resist another frenchification, and *croquer le bout de la baguette*. Bite the end off the bread.

SUMMER

JUNE

We drove down to Cognac yesterday. Road signs on the thirty-kilometre journey to the capital of brandy-manufacture were hardly required. We just followed the sun and the increasing congregation of vineyards. On the D731, outside Cognac, the vineyards reach the horizon.

The day out in Cognac was a bit of a busman's day trip; to restart the production of *pineau*, the local fortified wine made from fermented grape must and cognac, down in the *cave* of our Charentais house would be pleasingly authentic. At the very least we would have a drink of guaranteed provenance and ungainsayable purity.

Anyway: we thought a tour of the Hennessy plant in Cognac would be worthwhile. On catching sight of the grey, blocky factory, topped by a giant red Hennessy flag, on the quayside of the Charente, my daughter, Freda, commented, 'Looks like something from Stalin's Russia.' And the juxtaposition of the Charente was cruel to Hennessy; the Charente, chartreuse and elegant, is France's most beautiful river.

The first stop on the Hennessy tour was a former 'cellar' which, contrary to definition, was an above-ground pebble-dashed warehouse. The inside was given over to a slick, hi-tech lightshow ('digital immersion') demonstrating Hennessy's history since its foundation by Irish strong-arm mercenary

Richard Hennessy in 1765. A rap star would have loved it. Indeed, the US rap scene seems a target market for the brand.

When I was a child cognac was an after-dinner drink, taken with a Romeo y Julieta cigar, by gentlemen of a certain girth and age. Such as my father. Today, apparently, it is quaffed by Drake and other rappers with attitude.

Anyway: next we followed Gwen, our guide, across a gravel yard to a working 'cellar' – and into a state of beatitude. The cellar was long and wide and high with rows of oaken barrels, each filled with 'eau de vie', the distilled grape juice that is the basis of brandy. The barrels are permeable: they let air in, the vapour of eau de vie out.

Oh, the smell of it. Fruity. Intoxicating. Heavenly. About 3 per cent of each barrel evaporates, what brandy-makers call 'the angels' share'.

In that immense, shadowy cellar we witnessed and we nosed the beauty in brandy-making: the craft of the cooper; the know-how of the cellarman; the exquisite palate of the taster. All of them human things. *Savoir-faire*, you might say.

There was not a single electronic gimmick or gauge in sight for the actual making of the amber liquid. At Hennessy the product is still made by hand and by tongue, same as it ever was.

We came away enthused.

Thus, this bright summer's morning, I've stepped out into our vines, as keen as the razor-edge on my pruning knife. This year our most productive vines will be the mature Folle Blanche we inherited, which grow, their trunks as thick and gnarled as ship-rope wrists, along the stone wall of the garden.

Another of my misconceptions before sojourning in La Belle France, was that vines were low-maintenance fruit; in the growing season they are as needy as children, constantly requiring tying up to the trellis, trimming, and, like today, thinning of the leaves and shoots so that the grapes get adequate sunlight and ventilation to preserve their health.

Vines are delicate wards. Our vines have survived the Great Cold of May, when the thermometer plummeted to break regional records fifty years old. But who knows what weather awaits next week, next month? Last year the Charente department endured a May gale which left the vineyards, in the words of *Sud Ouest*, 'un triste spectacle'. After the storm came drought. Growing grapes is a game for optimists, for dreamers. In the spirit of hope I carry on working the healing-knife deep among the Folle Blanche foliage, rampant and wild. A steady pile of vines leaves accumulates beside me. At lunchtime I, wholly in touch with my inner transnational peasant ('Waste not, want not'), will use these to wrap and bake dolmades of rice and herbs. Again.

There was a shower in the night, and the fecund clusters of hanging miniature grapes, wet and green, are luscious in the rising heat. The naked earth around the base of the vines has the sweet warmth of baby's skin.

A red admiral butterfly fixes to the wall to dry its wings. A skylark rings silver notes above me. A twenty-two-spotted ladybird walks over my hand.

If Dionysus himself emerges from the vines it would be Arcady.

~

In all the kit and paraphernalia we have shipped over from England to France, the Lister electric sheep shears have got lost. An inquiry at the agricultural merchant in Chefnay about purchasing something similar engenders – after much *Ça va?*-ing, from the phlegmatic, bearded Jérôme and his assistants – a sucking-in of breath, a blowing-out of breath. 'We could order, but it would be a week. Maybe two . . .' The price would cover a weekend at the Georges V in Paris. This is not sheep country; only two other people in the village have sheep, and their 'flocks' are similar in size to mine. I am, frankly, in a panic; Serge, Sacha, Johnny, Max and Mini, stuck in their wool coats, are hot, keeping under the trees, only grazing by night. Too hot. And the thermometer is going one way only, up. So I drive over to Intermarché on the Zone Artisanale at Chefnay, and buy a BaByliss Men Face/Beard 6-in-1 Multi Trimmer for € 16.95. While I am certain that BaByliss will never include this in their advertising, the trimmer on a 5mm head produces, in the relative cool of that evening, one of the best shearings I have managed in twenty-five years of shepherding. The black wool comes off seamlessly, the sheep barely notice the procedure. For good measure, I bring the donkey into the entrance of the hay barn too, and trim her out. This is about 8 p.m.; and now I just sit here on the stone floor with my sheep and my donkey, talking to them, giving them treats of oats, my clothes smelling of lanolin, sweat and muck. In front of us, a paddock in full flower. Nothing in the world 'ancientizes' a scene like sheep and a donkey, particularly if you are so intimate with them that you know them by name, and they speak back. It could be a scene from Marcel Pagnol's 1963 novel *Jean de Florette*.

~

Later, in the evening, I discover Tris, my son, using the BaByliss for a DIY haircut; personally I prefer to visit Total Coiff, the unisex hair salon in Chefnay. French women spend an awful lot of time at the hairdresser, the net result of which is a national high standard in hair-cutting. Madame Lisianne at Total Coiff is a veritable artiste with her scissors. We have a routine: I approach the chair and say my hair looks like a *nid d'oiseau*, she smiles, strokes her pearl necklace thoughtfully, and then effects a sculpted miracle with flashing steel. Like the other customers, I sit in a state of beatitude. Total Coiff is a little temple of bliss.

~

I went for a tramp last night, partly for pleasure, partly from duty; the dogs needed their constitutional. Of course, this close to Midsummer, the land was not wholly dark at 9.30 p.m. – on the contrary, it seemed lit from within – but black enough for the familiar to become strange. Florets of elderflower hovered like a host of flying saucers, and white moths shuttled in the style of envoys from the court of the Faerie Queen. At the top of the track, just by the black-tunnel entrance to the wood, something flicked across my vision; my first thought was 'bat' . . . and then I registered that the flight style was not that of a wind-blown leaf, but was altogether more dynamic. More hawkish.

The nightjar cut a jig across the red band of the horizon, before becoming submerged in the darkness of the trees. I took this to be my allotment of nightjar-spotting, but on the way home I saw the nightjar – or its mate – twisting silently through the pale, stone-hued Limousin cattle of Guillaume Roban. The local name for the nightjar, *tête-chèvre*, reflects the European-wide superstition that the bird sucked the milk of goats.

When we bought the house from Madame Jacques, we also bought some of the furniture and effects. They seemed to belong here, and Madame Jacques agreed. Anything we wanted we stuck a yellow Post-it note on. The oak dining-room table, the

exquisite nineteenth-century chinoiserie buffet with its carvings, and the capacious chestnut wardrobes were obvious
choices. To the befuddlement of the estate agent, Paul Picard, I
was equally passionate about the 1970s clock in the kitchen,
which on the hour reproduces a particular bird's song. 'But,' he
said, 'you can buy those clocks for a few euros.'

True. Yet the clock on the wall was an expression of love for
birds, and I wished the house and the Jacques family to know
we too would cherish the birds. Last night, as I walked into
the kitchen, the clock struck ten. The electronic birdsong for
the hour was the purring of *l'engoulevent*. The nightjar.

Among the other furniture we bought from Madame
Jacques were three antique, wooden boat beds, all ornate carved
walnut. (We were amused on visiting the furniture exhibition
in the Musée des Cordeliers in Saint-Jean-d'Angély; the exhib-
its all seemed to come from our house.) However, we need a
new bed for the spare room, and buying a bed in France is
another of those cultural experiences that remind one that
France is a far-off land all by itself. In Britain, one buys a bed
and a mattress. In France, one buys the mattress and the bed
frame, but crucially the bed base, *le sommier*, is a separate purchase. Legion are the expats who have spent the night with the
new mattress on the floor. One acquaintance endured a double
whammy of *vive la différence*. On Epiphany, 6 January, he
argued over the phone with Camif, the furniture maker, for an
hour over the 'missing' bed base, and then settled down for a
reviving cup of tea, and a slice of Galette des Rois, a frangipane-
filled pastry traditionally eaten in France to mark the arrival of
the Three Wise Men in Bethlehem. What nobody had told him
was that within the pastry nestles a porcelain charm known as
the *fève*. So he broke a tooth.

We consoled him by pointing out he had avoided a crucial French custom to welcome the New Year. His car still existed. On New Year's Eve 2019 no fewer than 1,316 cars were put to the torch in France by jolly revellers. Stealing the shutters off a house also passes as a traditional way of celebrating the New Year across the Channel.

~

A *folie à un*. I'm on the phone to Auntie Marg, who lives in Leominster. 'What do you miss about England?' she asks. Spontaneously, I answer, 'Country pubs.' A second later, I add, 'Hopyards.'

I grew up with hop-farming; I cannot get it out of my system. Cannot.

The Charente is about as far from ideal hop territory as one can find; hops prefer slightly acidic, slightly moist clay soil. The sandy, brown limestone dirt of La Roche barely contains moisture, unless compacted, when it becomes concrete and the rain lies in long maudlin puddles. We are, however, our eccentricities. Ten minutes after putting down the phone to Auntie Marg, I have purchased, over the internet, ten rootstocks of Prima Donna, a dwarf hop, from Hopstock in northern France.

For my row of hops I dig out a trench three feet deep behind the courtyard wall, then build a foot-high stone wall to the front of the trench, and fill the ditch with my trusty well-rotted manure. Certainly, I quite fancy making beer (bittering with hops is what defines English beer), more certainly I will pick the excess hop shoots as a vegetable, and use the cones for a herbal sleep remedy. The hops arrive via a courier. Unpacked from their plastic, they are not unlike a particularly well-tentacled squid.

I plant them. And hope.

Five a.m. on 6 June, and the summer wake-up call of the

Charente: the persistent mewing of a mosquito, and I almost instinctively reach for my electronic racquet for swatting *les moustiques*, purchased from Intermarché's 'Kill Insects!' stand. I was once bitten by the invasive tiger mosquito, and my arm swelled to the size of my leg. Native to the tropical forests of South East Asia, *Aedes albopictus* has pied livery and is the vector of diseases such as dengue, chikungunya and Zika. It is now present in sixty-seven departments of the Hexagon.

The newspapers are full of the catastrophic decline of insects across the globe, with some experts suggesting the insect biomass has declined by 70 per cent in as many years. I can only say that in our small world of eastern Charente-Maritime, insect numbers are holding up; my sister-in-law stayed at a gîte nearby last year, and the first item in the 'Welcome Guide' was 'You may notice more insects here than in the UK', and instructions where to find mosquito-repellent devices, flypapers, etc. followed. (By the same token when Penny and I staffed the *buvette* at a village fête, some English attendees looked aghast at the black flies on the *galette;* Jean-François gave a Gallic shrug: 'Les Anglais n'aiment pas les mouches.') If we drive to Angoulême, our nearest big city, the grille of the car becomes a prop for *The Texas Chainsaw Massacre*.

So far, I have kept the red mite, the *poux rouges*, infestation of the chicken houses under control by lovely means; aside from the *pyrèthre végétal*, sprays of essential oils, including my own lavender. So far.

Not yet six in the morning. The village cockerels crow, but few if any humans, except farmers and gardeners, stir in the discarding of night. Yesterday the mercury went over 30°C, and I am watering the wilted *potager* before the scorching of the sun. While I am hosing the tomatoes, out of the hay barn three redstart fledglings fly. After dowsing the *potager*, I pick 2kg of green beans. As I did yesterday, and the day before. The family, at dinner, make sarcastic noises, 'Green beans! Such a surprise.' I have now invented the 'bean course', to go before the palate cleanser. I have forewarned the family about the burgeoning crop of purple beans.

The lavender has put on a foot of growth in a week.

~

Midday: squinting white heat, the air thick with the chainsaw buzz of cicada in the trees; the insect only starts its singing at 22–23°C. This morning I sow quarter of an acre of the brookside field with sunflowers (food for hens, sunflower oil for humans), and intend to continue my day by harvesting the garlic planted last November, but with mercury hitting 35°C I knock off for lunch at two minutes past twelve. Then stay indoors, for two hours, with the shutters nearly closed on the special latch which allows in a thin vertical slit of light, and air. When Guillaume Roban's tractor goes past at two minutes past two I recommence work.

~

Things I have not thought through about peasant farming in France, Number 10. Having lifted 15kg of garlic, how does one dry the bulbs? Eventually, I hit on the idea of running coir rope from one wall of the hay barn to the other, and back, and tie the bulbs to the rope; it looks as though a city of gnomes have strung out baggy underwear. After a week the bulbs (disappointingly gnome-sized, to be frank) are dried, and I make a vat of aioli, garlic mayonnaise, using our own hens' eggs. The recipe is authentic, passed to me by Jean-François's wife, Géraldine, who got it from her mother, who got it from her mother. The mausoleum of the Villier family in La Roche's cemetery dates to 1820. Which is about when the recipe was first written.

Aioli

6 garlic cloves, green germ removed
1 tsp sea salt
2 tsp Dijon mustard
3 large egg yolks
2 cups (500ml) grapeseed or other neutral oil
½ cup (120ml) fine quality, extra-virgin olive oil
2–3 tsp freshly squeezed lemon juice

Make a paste of the garlic and salt in a mortar with a pestle. Whisk in the mustard and egg yolks until they are blended with the garlic and salt. Then add ¼ cup (60ml) of the oil very slowly in a fine stream, and mix with the pestle; don't add the oil too quickly or the mixture will not emulsify.

Add one teaspoon of the lemon juice to the oil and garlic mixture, then add the remaining oil very slowly, turning the pestle constantly. The aioli will gradually thicken to the consistency of a light mayonnaise. Adjust the seasoning, and add more lemon juice if it needs more tang. If it becomes very, very thick you might add one tablespoon of warm water to loosen it.

Aioli will keep for several days in the refrigerator, in an airtight container, but is best served within twenty-four hours of being made.

A knock at the front gate, which is solid, set in in an arch of a high stone wall, so opening it can reveal the unexpected. This morning, it is Bernard Richard, who shuffles in, and asks, 'Would you like to visit our *truffière*?'

An afternoon later, the sky white and blinding, we drive out to the Richards' *truffière*, the route thoughtfully indicated by hasty hand-drawn signs stuck along the tracks and lanes. There are two other couples here, our retired doctor friends Louis and Marianne, and the Philippots, the young couple who run the village garage. It is an occasion, the women with their hair done (French women really do spend a lot of time at the *coiffeuse*), the men in the Ralph Lauren/Lacoste/Fred Perry polo shirts that are de rigueur as 'smart casual' in deep France.

The Richards show us around their long, serried rows of pubescent oak (*Quercus pubescens*), few of the trees more than twenty feet tall, and every one of them planted, back-breakingly, by the old couple themselves in the last twenty years. Such is the mystique of truffles that you forget that any truffle on your plate is as likely to be grown in a *truffière* as it is to be hunted down in a misty, ancient forest by a lonely woodsman with a pig on a rope. There are twenty thousand truffle farmers in France, where truffle orchards have been established for nearly two hundred years, starting with Auguste Rousseau's hectare of oaks in 1847.

Since our visit to the Richards' *truffière* is outside the moist harvest-time of south-west France for Périgord black truffles (November–March), Antoinette stages a spectacle: her achingly cute (and worryingly senescent) wire-haired terrier, Cora, detects a pre-planted truffle down in the chalky earth around the base of a tree in return for a bit of Emmental. The truffle is then excavated by Antoinette with a hand trowel.

The evolutionary trick of truffles is that they stink, alluringly so. They are pungent enough to penetrate layers of earth, and then distinguish themselves amid the surface olfactory cacophony. Thus, excited beasts dig them up, devour them, defecate their spores elsewhere. Truffles with better 'chemistry' will attract animals more successfully than those with worse. They will attract more money, too, if the said animals are *Homo sapiens sapiens* with gastronomic inclinations.

Someone, I forget who, articulates the question so obvious it is almost overlooked: 'How do you know the trees will produce truffles?' To which Antoinette replies, in a blasé tone suggesting an answer only necessary to infants, 'You buy the trees impregnated with truffle mycorrhiza. Some suppliers are better than others . . .' Shrug.

We retire to a long table covered with red-and-white check cloth, under the merciful shade of trees. The Richards have prepared truffle treats for us: *beurre de truffes* (¼ fresh grated truffle to ¾ salted butter, on toasted baguette), cold truffle omelette, truffle cheese – a sandwich of ripe brie ('pas trop fait', not too ripe) with layers of mashed truffle. An exhibition black truffle the size of a satsuma, sealed inside a small plastic food bag, to avoid the contamination of touch, is passed around the table. Truffles are not pretty. The word for truffle in many languages translates to 'testicle', as in the Old Castilian *turmas de tierra*. Earth's balls.

This afternoon, a *vin rouge de pays* in hand, a spore of an idea planted itself in our heads.

It's the trees, stupid. Where you can plant trees, you can have truffles, and I had been pondering how to fill an exposed stretch of land alongside our lane. Why not plant our very own mini-*truffière*? Every box ticked! Aesthetically satisfying. Potential money-earner, or at least a possible table treat. Shelter for the chickens.

If pubescent oak is the standard arboreal host for *Tuber melanosporum*, it is not the only one. Green oak, Austrian oak, kermes oak, lime, hazel and hornbeam are all alternatives. Following the old wisdom of 'Plant what grows naturally locally', we decide to order from a truffle tree nursery six one-year hazel whips mycorrhized with *Tuber melanosporum*, plus one pubescent oak so inoculated.

Before ordering the mycorrhized whips from Pépinières Robin I decide to make a coffee. Strolling into the kitchen – pleasantly bathed in warm sunlight through the open door to the courtyard – I find Rupert, the Border terrier, crouched by the side of the oven, absolutely immobile. Thinking he had espied a beetle or a spider, two of his favourite beings to hunt, I leaned down ... and found myself eye to eye with a coiled snake. With absolutely no cool at all, I shouted to the household, 'There's a bloody great snake in the kitchen!'

Penny appeared, looked at the serpent, and said, 'Isn't it beautiful?', which I thought was rather not the point. She called the rest of the household down to look at 'the lovely snake in the kitchen', before turning to me to ask, 'What sort of snake is it?' By now I had discovered some entirely appropriate sangfroid. 'It's a whip snake,' I replied. 'In French "couleuvre verte et jaune". They aren't poisonous, but they will bite if threatened.' By now the entire family had assembled, and the snake, tiring of the admiring attention, slid, as smooth as oil, under the *poêle*, the oil-heater. How does one remove a snake from a kitchen? Wild Tarzan-type thoughts of grabbing it behind the neck, or pinning it with a forked stick (a forked tool for a forked thing) possessed for me a second before I grabbed a broom, and banged on the side of the *poêle*, at which the snake stuck out its head, and bit the end of the broom.

'Wow,' chorused the assembled audience. Trying a gentler approach, I slid the thin end of the broom under the *poêle*, at which the snake shot out and went through the open door into the courtyard. We were all hot on its tail, wondering where it would go, but it disappeared into thin air. If we were awed by the snake's beauty, speed and vanishing act, I noticed that some of us wore boots in the kitchen, and generally edged around the furniture for days afterwards.

~

20 June. The Agediss courier delivers the box of hazel whips from Pépinières Robin. (Cost for the lot: one hundred and thirty euros, including P&P.) I spent yesterday running over the planting ground – at the end of a paddock, by the lane, the Pubert rotavator loosening the soil to 20cm, was the sole preparation before insertion this morning.

Our dirt, being calcareous, is beloved of black truffles (although not by our kitchen kettle); it will be five years at least before our truffle trees bear a harvest, which should be sufficient time to train our dog to sniff out the black subterranean nuggets, even if she is a daffy black Labrador. For the producer of truffles, a dog is an essential accessory.

Or a pig.

~

How still the Robans' barley field is at dusk. Not a breath of breeze. A scene trapped in a bottle.

Nothing moves in the heat, except a feeling of content, which grows to reach the hills.

At the very bottom of the valley where the wheat was cut yesterday, a red-legged partridge calls, that silly mechanical noise they make, like a car engine failing to start, over and over. The more this shallow valley fills with aqueous darkness, the more the wheat field seems to be running with milk. Beside me, the dog flops on her belly, panting and loll-tongued. The stars rise. The flower-heads of the wild carrot in the verge lumine, the white campion patch in the paddock is a doppel-gänger for a constellation of fallen stars. I'm checking the electric fencing posts – in the dry soil they constantly loosen – and by my foot there is a piercing spot of white light, such as you get if you refract sunshine through a magnifying glass.

A glow-worm (*Lamprohiza splendidula*). I'd always assumed, from the photographic evidence, that the light-emitting area was the rump; in fact, there are three bars on the abdomen which illuminate like miniature strip lights.

JULY

Our front lawn is a spectacle, a mini-wildflower meadow, as riven with colour as if Rider Haggard's Allan Quatermain had reached into King Solomon's treasure box and cast its jewels with mad, laughing abandon. A rare overnight deluge has made the lawn spangle and sparkle.

It needs cutting, and it will make fine hay for the horse and the donkey; they need it. Whereas in Britain one feeds hay to animals in winter when the grass has stopped growing, in the Charente one feeds the hay in summer, when the sun-blasted, browned-off grass has stopped growing. It is an inversion of haymaking my head never quite comprehends.

I have just purchased a galvanized hay rack with a roof; the roof is not to keep the rain off the hay, but the sun, which bleaches the hay and diminishes its palatability and nutritional content.

My scythe is the Grim Reaper sort, made though of light-weight tubular metal, rather than traditional ash wood. There is a certain amount of rigmarole in setting up a scythe: attaching the blade to the snath, checking the hafting angle . . . but the terminology is a compensation, full and satisfying as it rolls around the mouth.

It takes me a while to 'peen' (sharpen) the blade with the

whetstone. My father and grandfather could, with a Zorro flick of the wrist, give you an edge on steel you could shave with, be it a scythe or the Sunday carving knife. I was born too late for such superman skills; as for my children, I threaten to send them off to carving school. (Such places exist.)

Thus it is a good half-hour spent in the potting shed, where we also keep all the tools, before I start on the lawn; one man off to mow a mini-meadow.

To scythe grass, you want to start in the morning, after the moisture of the night has condensed on the green blades. A little wetness on the grass gives a grippy heaviness that facilitates cutting. You want to see the glint of sunlight on dew. Except, in the Charente, in the resumed *canicule* (heat wave), there is not a hint of dew on grass. A lot of watering is necessary in this land of little rain. Aside from the mains water, we have a well (so deep one can scarcely see the bottom, even with a torch), and the cistern, though the cistern brings its own problems, being the main breeding water for the mosquitoes. The Jacques family tried to deter said insects by planting lavender around the cistern; the lavender at least nectars the bumblebees, velvet carpenter bees, butterflies (predominantly meadow brown, painted lady, cabbage white), rosemary beetles and hummingbird hawk-moths. The hummingbird hawk-moths have no need to perch, a footloose, fancy freedom which makes more flowers available; hummingbirds, via convergent evolution, have the same technique. I'm placing my hope in the battle against the mosquitoes with great diving beetles, who are voracious consumers of mosquito larvae. *On y va*, anyway.

For a minute, I am at sixes and sevens, even eights and nines, before I get into the literal swing of scything; of bringing the blade – dead level, a millimetre off the ground – in a 180 degree arc, from right to left.

Then I am off. Lost in a trance. In a fugue. Into an altered state.

The scyther sees things others will never see. A sweep of my blade reveals the tubeway tunnels of voles through the grass; another sweep a black hole for a slow worm. Whispering, restless, the blade lobotomizes a meadow ants' nest, exposing its brain-like workings.

Swish-swish.

Scything is a lesson in entomology: the magnified sun, in its frictionless ascent of the blue dome, burns a hole through the fruit trees on the lawn. In the heat, I stop to rub the whetstone over the blade. (A palaver.) On my wellington, a dribble of white froth, from which a minute green fairy shrimp emerges – the naked nymph of the common frog hopper. The 'cuckoo spit' it makes by blowing bubbles from its anus is protection against predators.

Swish-swish.

Scything is a lesson in aesthetics: the fecund, heavy-headed seed heads of the grasses – rye, meadow fescue, wild oats, cocksfoot – possess a subtle, minimalist elegance, as though drawn by a Japanese sumi-e artist.

The old saying goes, 'Hay is always better with a bit of sweat on.' There is plenty of sweat on this hay; so dry are the grass and flowers that unless the blade is absolutely honed they bend before the blade, rather than being severed by it. By the time I finish the scything and put the tool down at around eleven, it is 27°C under the trees. The cicadas have started up, one a mere metre away in the rose bush beside the potting shed. The 'song' of the cicadas is one of the loudest any insect can produce; some can reach 90 decibels by flexing their 'timbal', a special membrane, at very high speed. (Unlike grasshoppers and crickets, which stridulate using their back legs.) It is a love song, used by the male to attract the female, and is the sound of summer in southern France. Below 22°C, the timbal diaphragm loses its elasticity, which is why the beige insect is quiet in rain, at night, and does not generally *chante* in the north.

In French the cicada is *la cigale*, and is synonymous with carefree insouciance, largely due to the fable 'La Cigale et la Fourmi' by Jean de la Fontaine (1621–95). This features a thrifty, hardworking little ant who spends his summer collecting food for 'when the north wind doth blow', and the happy-go-lucky cicada who does nothing but 'sing her song all summer long'.

When winter comes, the cicada goes begging to her neighbour the ant 'for a little grain 'til summer comes back again'. The ant in the fable, however, being self-righteous and stingy, replies, 'You sang, did you?' . . . 'Well, dance now!'

~

If France's sense of itself is rooted in the land, tensions between city and country manifest. The sound of cicadas and other rural noises have not been to the liking of visitors and incomers; a few years ago, the mayor of Beausset, near Toulon, was asked by holidaymakers to kill *les cigales* with insecticide.

In 2019 second-home owners on the Île d'Oléron, off the west coast, brought a case against a cockerel, Maurice, for crowing too early. But the rural French are vigilant, militant. Thousands of people signed a 'Save Maurice' petition, and a judge eventually upheld the cock-a-doodle-doos, ordering the plaintiffs to pay one thousand euros in damages to Maurice's owner, Corinne Fesseau. After a host of similar cases in which an unholy trinity of 'néo-ruraux', Brit expats and holidaying Parisians complained about the loud and smelly ways of France *profonde*, the National Assembly backed a bill from Pierre Morel-À-L'Huissier, a deputy from the Lozère, to protect France's 'sensory heritage', meaning 'the crowing of the cockerel, the noise of cicadas, the odour of manure'. *Ça marche, pour moi.*

～

Another July morning, and the heat is on. In the *potager* I harvest, with secateurs and shears, rosemary, sage, parsley, thyme, lemon thyme, tarragon, vervain, lemon balm, sorrel (green and red), chives, savory, curry plant, mint, parsley, flat-leaved parsley, absinthe. But not coriander. I do not know what I do wrong, but if I so much as look at coriander I kill it. Nonetheless, quite a herby haul, strung up on wire lines between woodshed and garage to dry. Then the cleaning of preserving jars out on the front lawn, sitting under the scented, flowering limes, as abuzz with noise as an F1 Grand Prix heard over a hill. In the squinting white heat, a turtle dove coos down the chimney into my study, which acts as a sound box; the noise comes out through the open windows to waft around my ears.

The postmistress's yellow Berlingo van pulls up in a bellow of chalk dust, and she peeps the horn. 'Bonjour, madame. Ça va?' I say on opening the front gate. She, red-faced, fans herself with our post, before passing the handful of letters through the window. 'Phew. Forty degrees down in the village,' she exclaims, pointing at the thermometer on the dashboard. Here it is 35°C, and hot enough. The dog's bowl is rimmed with wasps and goldfinches drinking the water. I wish her 'Bonne journée.' She replies, 'Également.' Equally.

Out of the window, as she reverses, she points, laughing, at the envelopes.

Merde. Putain, Fait chier. Bordel. Salope. Putain de merde ...
Another speeding fine.

~

10 July: I was intending to begin the lavender harvest yesterday, but the Robans were cutting their wheat, and the combine
threw up great clouds of dust. A white-out. The heads of lavender bow with the weight of the insects; I took a few snips
anyway, rubbed them over my arms and face to keep away the
mosquitoes, and dunked the rest in water; in the afternoon, the
nuclear sun rising, I sprayed the mixture over Zeb and Snowdrop as fly repellent.

So today, after the dew had dried, I started on the lavender
with the petrol hedge cutter. (A lavender harvest is no dainty
tea-picking affair; ours is done with a Husqvarna 522HDR60X.)
Despite the ditty's claim 'Lavender's blue, dilly dilly', lavender
vraie is actually a washed-out mauve. Insects love the plant;
almost every head was ornamented by a bee or a butterfly.
(I left a tenth of every lavender bush uncut; a sort of tithe
for Nature.) The petrol hedge cutter was brutally, loudly effi-
cient; the perfume of the tumbling lavender towers was
intoxicating.

Like any harvest, that of lavender is a matter of just-right
timing; when harvesting lavender for dried buds to use in potpourri, sachets or culinary uses, one harvests when 25–50 per
cent of the buds are blooming. Like today. If I were harvesting
lavender for essential oil distillation, I would wait until 50–100
per cent of the buds are blooming.

Lavender loses its oil to the heat of the day, so one harvests in
the cool of the morning (before 10 a.m.) so the cut lavender has
a higher oil content.

After harvesting the thirty bushes, I laid out the stalks to dry on a 20m² tarpaulin as blue as the sky.

~

Kingsley Amis considered the most dreaded phrase in life to be 'Red or white wine?' although, for me, 'Shall we visit an aquatic plant nursery?' runs it close. Those tubs of samey pondweed, the tanks of koi, with their ceaseless mouths.

However, we required water lilies for the cistern for decoration, for shade – so that the invertebrates do not broil alive – and also to keep the mosquitoes under control; theoretically, the leaves of the lilies reduce the amount of surface area in the cistern available for the female of the mosquito species to lay her eggs.

If you live in France, there is only one place to buy water lilies, and that is the nursery and garden of Latour-Marliac, which is the birth pool of the coloured hardy water lily – and also nothing less than the birth pool of Claude Monet's greatest paintings. It is where Monet bought his lilies. So, not your usual aquatic plant nursery. Accordingly, we did not drive the hundred miles even further south to the Lot-et-Garonne department in wholly sceptical mode; painting and garden history press the family's particular pleasure buttons.

There is Paul's conversion on the road to Damascus; then there is our walk around the Art Nouveau stone rectangular and circular pools of Latour-Marliac. We exited en famille, adults and young adults alike, clasping polythene bags of nymphaea and as confirmed water lily cultists. For the first time in my life I understood obsession with a single plant species. Some have orchid-mania; I now suffer nymphaea-mania.

The water lily nursery was founded in 1875 by Joseph Bory

Latour-Marliac, the scion of a local estate owner, on ten acres of Arcadia bursting with two wells, a stream and fourteen springs. At the time the only hardy water lily in Europe was the plain white *Nymphaea alba*. Through a process of hybridization akin to alchemy, Latour-Marliac crossed hardies with tropicals to construct a water lily palette ranging from alp-white to midnight-purple, via yellow, copper, red and at least forty shades of pink. (Water lilies, I can confirm, look particularly pretty in pink.) In 1889 Latour-Marliac exhibited his novel water lily collection at the World Fair in Paris; from that exhilarating climax of the Belle Époque, only two French monuments now survive, the Eiffel Tower and Latour-Marliac's lilies. The nursery Latour-Marliac founded outside the *charmante* town of Le Temple-sur-Lot is now a state-approved 'Jardin Remarquable', and the water lily the unofficial floral emblem of the Republic.

It was at the Paris Exposition Universelle that Latour-Marliac's coloured water lilies, displayed in the Trocadéro, caught the painterly eye of Claude Monet, who was exhibiting in the nearby Pavillon des Artistes. Via mail order Monet commanded box loads of the new-fangled plants for his *jardin d'eau* at Giverny, north-west of Paris. The rest is art history: the water lilies became the subject of over two hundred mesmeric, paradigmatic paintings. With a commercial instinct not then associated with art, Monet severely restricted access to his floating floral treasures at Giverny. He created a waterscape, and he kept it as his own. Monet enshrined the water lily in his art.

Monsieur Latour-Marliac had other equally enthusiastic and influential customers. To be found in the company archives are orders from Baroness Orczy, the Vatican, the King of Bulgaria and Tolstoy. What truly fertilized the company's early growth, however, was its fan base in Great Britain. William Robinson, the founder of *Garden* magazine, was an early champion of Latour-Marliac's water lilies; the forty-fourth volume (1894) was dedicated to 'Mons. B. Latour-Marliac, who has brought the lovely colours and forms of the water lilies of the East to the waters of the North'. Gertrude Jekyll was another fervent supporter, and had a blooming pen-friendship with the water lily man; in reply, Latour-Marliac simply and elegantly addressed the gardening sage as 'Mademoiselle'. James Hudson, head gardener at Leopold de Rothschild's Gunnersbury Park, was a regular customer, and had the honour of having a water lily named after him, *N.* 'James Hudson'. By 1904, some 75 per cent of Latour-Marliac's business was from the other, greyer side of the Channel.

Some of the ephemera of the near hundred and fifty years of the Latour-Marliac enterprise, including a two-page, neat scroll order from Monet himself, are exhibited in the small museum at the nursery, housed in a former plum oven on a small bluff overlooking a grotto, waterfall, tropical glasshouse with giant water lilies, and lake complete with arching Japanese bridge – an honourable nod in steel to Monet. Adjacent to the *musée* is the convenient Café Marliacea, which sells a 50cl *pichet* of decent, refreshing white wine for nine euros (this also is wine country, after all), while you seek shade from the sun of south-west France under the vine-roofed pergola, drink in the views of Latour-Marliac's water wonderland in its verdant valley, and ponder what to purchase.

The buyer of Latour-Marliac water lilies is faced with an *embarras du choix*. We expected aesthetics, but – because we were only familiar with common *Nymphaea alba* – we had not expected the swooning perfumes of M. Latour-Marliac's great gifts to gardening. The sense of smell is the sense most difficult to vocabularize, so we fell back on the winemakers' lexicon, with its notes of 'intense orange', 'floral', 'candy'.

Undecided, we five – my foursome family plus Tris's *petite amie* – returned to the grid of rectangular exhibition pools, a giant aquatic paint box, and dreamily sniffed the exotic fragrances. Dragonflies and darters added their dash of colour to the colour scene, and frogs plopped lazily off the shiny floating plate-leaves into the water. (Frogs and water lilies go together like horse and carriage, and, if you think about it, like long-limbed water lilies with Art Nouveau.) If only the surface of the pool into which Narcissus gazed had been replete with Latour-Marliac's chromatic star-bursts he would have seen something more gorgeous than himself.

Decisions had to be made. The temptation to throw all sense of taste away was rampant. The rest of us wanted coherent pink and white, but I had a strong weakness for the daffodil-yellow *N.* 'Marliacea Chromatella' and the midnight-bruised crimson of *N.* 'Black Princess'. In the end, tone – and intoxicating scent – won the afternoon. We chose the red *N.* 'Tan-Khwan' (with its nostalgic nose notes of sweetshop), the hot pink *N.* 'Mayla', and the pure white *N.* 'Hermine'; the flower of the latter is sharp, precisely geometric, apparently sculpted from ice. Such cold beauty, we felt, could cool our own sun-basted pond.

The water lilies of Latour-Marliac are not cheap (*N.* 'Tan-Khwan' is an eye-watering forty-nine euros per plant), but then one is paying for beauty, history and pondlife conservation in one floral package. And for art too, because are the exquisite water lilies of Latour-Marliac any less creatively brilliant than Monet's paintings of them? Or less than Hector Guimard's sinuous, full-budded wrought-iron Paris Métro entrances, which have always owed more to water lilies than lilies of the valley?

～

Personally, I used to consider the saddest phrase in the English language, 'You've missed the sun.' Now I could do with some English rain; every morning watering, watering before the sun blasts the flinching land. It seems absurd to be using mains water, when one has a well, so I finally order a submersible pump from Ouest Agro. How long before it arrives? Jérôme grimaces: 'A week . . . or two.'

～

I'm hazy about the exact time, but not long after two, I walk down into the village, which appears as a small sea of red terracotta roofs, set in vineyards and sunflower fields in a shallow valley, bounded by low hills and hard-topped by blue woods and rolling hills as far as the eye can see. On entering the village proper, I plunge into the white, man-made gorge of the Chemin du Loup, the houses tight to the cobbled stone lane, and whose name speaks of a time before the houses were even foundations. The winding *chemin*, ornamented by red valerian and hollyhocks in every opportunistic crevice in the ground, narrows as it enters the village centre. I have Rupert and Plum on tight leads; there is a tempting stray cat to chase lounging on every corner. The sun beats off the buildings; Monsieur Roban the Elder drives up past me on his tractor wearing mirrored sunglasses, which gives him a distinctly mafia look. I debouch out into the village by the *église*, and cut across the blinding village square to the brookside field.

Pulsating sun, sultry, nothing stirring, except for a desultory cabbage white butterfly; nothing sounding except for crickets in the long grass on the lane, and the cicadas in the trees. The birds, exhausted by breeding, have entered the great July silence. One bird only sings: a wood pigeon deep in a plane tree, 'roo-cooing' absent-mindedly, soporifically.

A countryside so stilled and breathless it seems trapped in a sequence of landscape portraits: pale Limousin cattle grouped under the parasol of an oak; the field of creamy, heavy-headed wheat awaiting cutting; the vineyard on the bank. And lastly, *The Field of Sunflowers*. Our sunflowers are six feet high, and zombie-gaze at the sun.

Like the sunflowers, my hops have grown like topsy, and twirly-whirled their way up the guiding strings, to fall back in jungly masses. There are more shoots than the plants need, so I gather about a third as a seasonal vegetable and poach one lot (half a kilo) in lemon water and serve up for the evening meal at 8 p.m.; this is now on five courses, with the addition of cheese and biscuits, and eaten outside under the trees – which is exactly how one imagines French life.

The remainder of the hops, a kilo and a half, I pickle in spicy vinegar. Pickled hop shoots are among the most expensive vegetables, at twenty euros a jar, one can find. I have arranged a barter with Monsieur Martin, who runs the charcuterie stall in Chefnay's street market, held every Wednesday and Sunday: two jars of pickled hops for a corn-fed dressed chicken *élevé en plein air*, by an old farmer he knows just over by Matha. So good is the chicken, apparently, it merits a 'chef's kiss', the gesture made by pinching the fingers and thumb of one hand together, kissing them, and then tossing them dramatically away from the mouth with a sighing 'Ahh!' Monsieur Martin reckons that hop shoots taste like asparagus, though with a bitter herbal kick. *Bon appétit*, we wish each other, deal done.

~

Late evening, 12 July. The lights of Guillaume's combine harvester on a distant hill cutting barley; faint lines of deer tracks through the wheat leading down to the brook, like watermarks on paper. The old country adage concerning the nightingale is that 'In May he sings both night and day, in June he altereth his tune, in July he'll fly away.' Certainly, I have not heard the bird for a week or more.

Freda and I take Zeb up to the wood, taking it in turns to ride him, along the trackways, lined with yellow flowers now, and also in the little fields lost among the trees. On the way back down the track to home I pull down a globular green walnut from the tree near the barn, and stamp it under my foot; there is no shell, the contents are white and milky. So the walnuts are still young enough to pick for the array of green walnut pickles and ketchups. (A more civilized testing method is to stick a pin in the nut; if you can feel a shell inside, discard. They must have an unformed shell.) By tradition green walnuts can be picked no later than 14 July, Bastille Day, but not before the feast day of Saint Jean, 24 June.

~

My peasant life: save for a two-hour break for lunch, I have spent the entire day picking green walnuts, the low-hanging fruit, not just from our trees, but the vast shadowy trees along the lanes of the village, putting the haul in the back of the van. An itinerant nut-collector. It was too hot to wear gloves, so the dye from the skin of the nuts has turned my hands coal-black.

On the bathroom scales, the two sacks weigh in at just under 45kg in total. The next day is swallowed by the preparatory work of pickling walnuts. But it was all done under the lime trees, listening to the cicadas, the breath of the wind in the leaves, watching the wood pigeons feed the squab.

Pickled Walnuts

115g salt
1kg green walnuts
500ml malt vinegar
250g brown sugar
1 tsp allspice
1 tsp cloves
½ tsp cinnamon
1 tbsp fresh ginger, grated

Dissolve the salt in the water to make a brine. Leave the nuts in the brine for seven days, then strain, drain and refresh the brine. Leave nuts submerged for another week. Drain, and dry on a rack for ten to twelve days. They will go black.

Mix the remaining ingredients to make a spiced pickling vinegar. Put the black walnuts in a jar, and cover with the spiced pickling vinegar.

After preparing thirty jars' worth of pickled walnuts, it did occur to me that maybe more could be done with the nuts? So I dug out a recipe for the traditional aperitif of walnut country, *vin de noix*, sweet and dark, and which is obtained by macerating walnuts in red wine and spirits, in my case cognac, from M. and Mme Gaillard's distillery in the nearby hamlet of Sainte-Hilaire. In the past the walnut 'wine' was known for its therapeutic qualities and considered a medicinal tonic, digestive and depurative.

Vin de Noix

3.5 litres red wine
1kg brown sugar
0.5 litre cognac
1 orange, cut into pieces
14 green walnuts, quartered
4 cloves

Mix all the ingredients in a big bowl, then place in a demijohn (*bonbonne*). Shake every day for forty days. Sieve the liquid into sterilized bottles, and cork. Drink at Noël.

Failing the above recipe, there is a venerable version based around the number four. To four litres of wine, add forty walnuts chopped into four, with forty cubes of sugar and a quarter of eau de vie (brandy), and mature for forty days.

～

14 July, Bastille Day. A public holiday. The sun is (of course) shining, and a communal midday meal has been organized in the small square off the centre of La Roche, in front of the church. Tipped off by Jean-François that the meal invariably ends with a rendition of 'La Marseillaise', the French national anthem, I have spent days learning the words by watching a subtitled You-Tube video of Mireille Mathieu, a raven-black-bobbed Marianne if ever there was one. I am a confident and proficient performer of verses one and six, which are generally the only ones sung. (Quite bloody, by the way, the words of the rousing, sing-along

French national anthem, when translated: 'To arms, citizens!/ Form your battalions/Let's march, let's march/That their impure blood/Should water our fields.') As is the way of communal meals in the village, we sit at long trestle tables under a *tivoli* (an open-sided marquee), eat four courses – today supplied by an outside caterer, from the village over the hill – which are served by village volunteers. There is red, white and rosé wine, gallons of it, plus orange juice and water. A merry, chattery time is had by all; we sit opposite a couple in their seventies who have a holiday home in La Roche, but originally hale from the commune; the talk is light and easy: gardening; the English couple in Pardeau who have done up their house 'to the nines'; and the number of feral felines about the place, who are fed, despite warnings from the *maire*, by the eccentric 'cat lady.' Coffee is served. Mentally, I run through the words of 'La Marseillaise'. I am ready. The *maire*, Alice Prudhomme, stands up. I start to push back my chair; she then announces that the entertainment will begin, at which a hired singer – of some age – accompanied by a guitarist of similar vintage walks on to the low wooden dais, plugging in a mike and an electric guitar to a Marshall amp, and launches into 'Emmenez-moi' by Charles Aznavour. No Marseillaise. Then again, 'Emmenez-moi' is a sort of French national anthem. Everyone, young and old, knows the words, myself included. My stepmother brought me up on Aznavour's 'Emmenez-moi' and 'La Bohème', plus Charles Trenet's 'La Mer', and Gilbert Bécaud's 'Et maintenant'. All of which happen to be the next songs sung. Everyone is singing, clapping along, swaying in unison from side to side on their benches, and a decent-sized contingent of the women – from the twenty-something daughter of the *maire* to the grand old hunchbacked lady in the slate-roofed house – is on the stage dancing. The

French are different to you and me. Less inhibited about public performance.

The two musicians perform their hearts out for an hour. But it is not enough for the village crowd. There is an encore. Another. Another. The entertainment goes on until late afternoon, at which everyone ambles off for a rest; there is a firework display in the nearby town at night.

Penny and I walk up the hill with our neighbours David and Claudine. I ask Claudine if she enjoyed the day, 'Ça vous a plu?' She replies, wagging a slightly wine-wobbly finger, 'John, I must correct your French. With me you should use the familiar. So, "Ça t'a plu?"'

~

17 July. Harvested the purple towers of wild marjoram (or oregano if it is an ingredient of Italian cooking) from our paddocks, but also from the verges of the lanes; Antoine, the village handyman, will be cutting them next week, so I am saving him work. At the top of the track, just below the wood, the verges flickered with marbled white butterflies, and I saw myself in a black-and-white film from the 1920s.

~

Sunday morning. Two teenage girls from the village, done up to the nines, strappy Roman sandals and make-up and jewellery, walk past the house arm-in-arm. I'm filling the equids' water trough with an extension to the hose across the track. They stop, say hello, call me 'Monsieur', ask about Zeb and Snowdrop, declare them 'mignons', and are utterly polite.

Ten minutes later, two elderly women, done up to the nines in floral dresses and jewellery, walk past the house arm-in-arm, stop, say hello, ask me about Zeb and Snowdrop, and are utterly polite.

Sometimes, I am utterly fazed by rural France. No one here has ever called me 'mate', and even toddlers look one in the eye and politely say, 'Bonjour, monsieur.' And as for dressing up for the Sunday walk? I think I remember it, circa 1970, in east Herefordshire with my grandmother. (Such a perambulation presumably followed Communion.) But then again, I seem to remember that Ferdinand Mount writes about the phenomenon in his memoir *Cold Cream*. Perhaps I am suffering false memory syndrome.

So, it is a rather bemused me that stands under the sanctuary of the spreading lime tree. Beyond the circle of shade, only heat haze and a dissolving world.

Despite the undulating air beyond the tree, there is a stillness to the land, as if it were stuck in a glass hot house; the sole sounds are the hacksawing of cicadas in the walnut orchard and the equally rhythmic, metallic clicking of my tree loppers.

I am cutting the lower fronds of the lime trees. Like the other limes planted in remote Charente in the nineteenth century, our limes were intended as multitasking working trees: to supply the house with shade, that welcome gloom, in summer, and to furnish wood for the home fires in winter. The same wood, easy to work and hard to split, would have been carved for toys, and cut for poles.

On and on go the historic French uses of *le tilleul*. The flowers fed the honeybees, flavoured drinks. In Alain-Fournier's 1913 novel *Le Grand Meaulnes,* a requiem-in-advance for lost idealism (the author himself was killed in the Great War), the schoolboy narrator recalls attic rooms 'where we kept drying lime leaves and ripening apples'.

The last significant use of lime's heart-shaped leaves was animal fodder, which is the reason I am chopping boughs off the tree on this July day. In northern Europe, cut and dried arboreal leaves were anciently stored for feeding to the animals during winter; in south-west France the hunger time is droughty July and August.

Looking up into the tree's depths for the right place to cut is a literal pain in the neck. And, of course, all falling branches stab my shoulder, while all the biting insects bite my neck, leaving me with a pearl-choker of bites.

Aphids, ants, firebugs, woodlice, beetles, fluorescent green caterpillars of the lime hawk-moth, nameless black flies, nameless green flies all shower down on me. Cutting trees for fodder is, of course, the best of all jobs. As Pliny the Elder noted, 'Nature is nowhere as great as in its smallest creatures.' When working under a tree one is very close to Nature.

This is the last batch of dried-leaf fodder for this summer; I have waited for the wood pigeon squab in the lime to fly its nest-raft of flotsam twigs, the black redstart young to quit their dark hole along a cranny, behind a gnarl. I have made so-called 'tree hay' from other limes, from maple, from ash; there is about a ton of the stuff hanging up in 'bales' in a shed to dry.

Today, in this fierce heat, the leaves are drying within hours of me simply throwing them out into the sunlight, which sears-in their minerals and nutrients. Their goodness.

Later, when carrying the lime boughs by the armful through the white light to the shed for storage, I launch one towards my horse. As the branch arcs the pure blue horizon it leaves a trail of scent; it is the same fabulous smell as a packet of China tea, fresh opened.

Zeb gobbles the sun-baked lime leaves in preference to

meadow sward. Thus, the ultimate proof of the utility and tastiness of tree hay comes direct from the horse's mouth.

~

Our Wednesday morning ritual: off to the street market in Chefnay, with its fish stall, *bio* veg stall, the flower stall run by the bouquet-creating *artiste* with scissors and ribbon, two cheese stalls, two clothes stalls for women (selling exquisite linen), the one stall for men's clothes (meaning blue work kit), the stall selling soaps, the stall selling rugs, the bike repair stall, the Vietnamese food stall, the stall selling *crêpes*, the garden plant stall, the chocolate stall, and Monsieur Martin's charcuterie stall. The town square is packed, it is heaving. The *bar-tabac* and the bistro have tables and chairs spread out into the sunshine. Starlings are chattering in the lime trees, people chattering around the stalls. It is magazine-photograph France, yet real France. We go principally for the fish stall, and queue alongside friends and neighbours, acquaintances. As I drive in, I spot a free parking place under the shading limes. Sometimes, one just cannot believe one's luck. I open the van door, almost knocking over a pile of wire crates belonging to a man selling poultry, a black Basque beret on his head, an unlit cigarette dangling from the corner of his mouth. He has chickens, he has ducks and, *mon dieu*, he has geese. Roman and Toulouse. All of his stock is in feather-glistening, bright-eyed condition. Within five minutes we have five Toulouse geese in cardboard boxes, air holes ripped in them with flashes of the seller's pocket Stanley knife. 'Do you want to bring your car up?' he asks. I touch the van. '*Vous aimez les oies, alors!*' he says, laughing.

Small-scale farming, subsisting on the product of one's own farm, requires livestock that are cheap and easy maintenance, and provide protein as well as cash. Such as geese. Toulouse, that old

French breed (the records go back to 1555), are famed for being the force-fed provider of foie gras. More to our taste is that Toulouse are reasonable layers, 25–40 extra-large white eggs per year, and if they don't beget golden eggs, they do beget white eggs that cooks rave about. Then there is their grease, and of course their bodies, eventually, roast with port wine gravy, or, for the mature bird, armagnac and a cast-iron casserole dish. I might even do something with their feather (goose down). Hell, I'll write with a quill.

Geese are also great improvers of the sward, they crop grass close, and frequently, with their precision serrated bills, stimulating growth; they are feathered lawn mowers, waddling muck-spreaders. More, geese also sound off like klaxons when any stranger approaches the property. (It was the sacred geese of Juno, by honking the alarm, that saved Rome from the Senone Gauls' surreptitious attack in 390 BC.) A goose adorns a farm. A goose wandering the farmyard and paddocks trails behind its tail feathers the absolute aura of traditional family farming in the same manner as sheep and donkeys. A goose (like a duck, a chicken, a goat or other small farm animal) is an agent of liberation. Give a person a goose/chicken/goat and they have their own food, a degree of independence.

These are some of my thoughts, as I release the geese, all of whom have been named even before they set webbed foot on our property. Coco, Geneviève, Céline, Charlotte and Catherine. Another thought is . . . everything above is justification. I just love geese. I like their company. They amuse me.

Released into the paddock beside the house, the geese waddle off at speed. The Toulouse is a deep-hulled bird with a big beam, and on the green grass-sea the geese momentarily appear as medieval ships a-sailing.

AUGUST

Cancan swirls of dust on the track. The horse paddock golden and sandy. When did it last rain? I cannot recall.

The old dovecot, mellow and stone, stands in the corner of the courtyard. From the north wind of winter the *colombier* is sheltered by the woodshed, while across the lane the store-house, now with its roof succumbed, protects the doves' home from the dusty, summer easterlies.

Father Jacques was a village *curé* unafraid of physical labour. Indeed, he seems to have loved working with his hands, and was rather good with them, as I am appreciating, having spent the last week refurbishing – pointing stone, rehanging doors, making wooden treads for the stairs, wire-brushing this, painting that of the dovecot.

I do not like DIY, except for the finishing of it. Still, the four-cornered tranquillity of the courtyard was soothing, the black redstarts and their funny snakey-rattle calls were companionable, the toffee wafts from the ripening sunflower fields were seductive, and the sky was blue and blinding. The only real markers of the gentle passage of the days were the thinning of the village's evening swirl of swifts, as the birds began their migration south, and the re-glorying of the dovecot.

The dovecot is an architectural, and an agricultural, wonder.

You get to know a man's mind when you mortar, paint and saw in his handprints. Father Jacques was, truly, as Bernard Richard said months ago, a curate with imagination: the square stone tower of the dovecot triples up as piggery and guinea-fowl house.

On the ground floor are a pair of pigsties; above them the guinea-fowl quarters with built-in nest boxes, which the birds reached by a wooden ramp, the humans by a wrought-iron ladder; topping the guinea-fowl gaff is a ring of square holes for the doves. All under a pitch, red-tile roof.

The dovecot looks *beau*. *Élégant*, even. Father Jacques had the fair eye of an aesthete, as well as the callused hands of a toiler. But most of all, the dovecot-cum-piggery-cum-coop is a perfect satisfaction of the old farming rule of the multiple usage of small space, in the same way that the apple orchards of my native Herefordshire once upon a time produced sheep and geese, in addition to the fruit. The dovecot is proper agricultural multitasking.

The doves, guinea-fowl and pigs, like Father Jacques, are long gone, though, in a sense, their good work lingers on too.

Stinging nettles give away the secrets of the past. *Urtica dioica* adores phosphate, which is abundant in manure heaps. When we took over Father Jacques's house, the courtyard wall of the dovecot had an attitudinous, imperious bed of nettles: they marked the site where, when the animal quarters were cleaned, Father Jacques dumped the waste.

In an extension to the dovecot of which I believe Father Jacques would approve, I have dug the nettles up – every rebirthing rhizome of them – and walled up the ex-midden to make a herb bed. Sage, parsley, rosemary, thyme, chives and lavender are already growing with fabulous ease.

But even such rich soil requires watering in a land of drought, where there is a hosepipe ban and Death comes not with a scythe but with a thermal lance. This year the thermometer has reached 40.5°C.

So the herb bed has been grateful for water from Father Jacques's cistern. Of course, being a curate with imagination, he saw that even the cistern might not provide enough water for his needs, so he dug a well too.

Down in the well's depths, you can see the original waters of the world form and flow. Today we dropped down the submersible pump from Agri Ouest, and up flowed the water, milky with calcium, and life-giving.

I tentatively suggest to the rest of the family the keeping of doves in the dovecot. Their silence is eloquent. I am the family hillbilly, give me an inch, and I'll turn it into a mile of down-home, backyard farming, a small empire of productive dirt, wool, flesh. And feathers. Turning the dovecot into a changing room for a plunge pool seems to be a more favoured option.

~

Everything comes early here; on 6 August we pick the plums, then blackberries, along the track. I finish the day by taking the dogs for a walk through the summer wood; round every corner of the rutted track is the expectation that some powder-wigged *comte* will come clattering along in a horse-drawn carriage. Out of the wood, and into the next Watteau tableau laid out before me: wheat field, woods and sunflowers, and the Robans' Limousin cattle, in their night field. On the skyline of the Robans' largest wheat field, a silhouetted family are walking home from a novel by Zola.

When I open the garden gate, perching on the *marquise*

above the front door is Speckledy Jim, a racing pigeon who sometimes sojourns with us, and who must be added to the list of house fauna.

The next day, in the oven-sun, I get out the briquette-making paraphernalia. It occurs to me now, as I pulp copies of *Sud Ouest*, that it is so much harder to note when birds stop their singing, as opposed to when they start. Is it a day or is it two weeks since the turtle doves last purred down the chimney? Behind me, in the stubble of the wheat, starlings fall like meteorite showers, and a single peregrine falcon 'chickers'. The wind is too strong today for flying insects, save for a solitary black bee, and one hummingbird hawk-moth in the lee of the stone wall.

On Sunday I cycle into town to buy the baguette, and am overtaken several times by pelotons of gaudy Lycra-clad people with drop-handled racing bikes; re-enactments of the Tour de France are a Sunday hazard hereabouts. The experience is not unlike being passed by a flock of parakeets.

A friend from England comes to visit, and we pick her up from Limoges airport. She works for an NGO; driving through western Charente, she says, 'This is actually more deserted than Ethiopia.' For miles there is not a house in sight, just woods and fields, fields and woods. In France, the countryside goes on for ever.

On the way to our house I drive through the town of Champagne-Mouton, chiefly for the pleasure of seeing its name on the red-edged sign beside the road; it is my favourite place name in the world, but then again I like sheep and I like champagne. (I am quite a toponymist; other favourite local place names are Brie, Gros Bonnet and Paizay-le-Tort, the latter meaning Paizay the Wrong.) At about 10 p.m. we reach our forest, and the spray of the car headlight catches a short-eared owl. 'Oh, I've seen an owl,' our friend says. By the time we arrive at the house, the local *hiboux* have put on a good display: she adds tawny, barn and little owls to her list.

The August lull in Nature; no birds singing, the lawn dry, the leaves of everything hardened, thick and literally moth-eaten. The weather suits the red mites; I believed I had them under control, but once again, the ashy smudges, and one or two bloody, pimply clusters in the hen houses. Alain, the neighbour who raises the cockfighting cockerels, purses his lips, and suggests wood-ash baths, so I hack out two 1m x 1m squares in the hens' paddocks, and fill them with wood ash. We have plenty of wood ash, since logs are our fuel in the bedrooms, as well as my study and the sitting room. My ash stash, which I usually use as potash in the *potager*, is a metre high.

~

The year on the slide to autumn, and more gloomy news. Under the cherry tree on the lawn, the corpse of a collared dove squab. This elegant avian from the Middle East is one of western Europe's most successful invaders, its trisyllabic 'doo-DOO-doo' now bouncing around chimney tops and farmyards across the lands. Collared doves become quite tame, perching in their pairs (they are monogamous) on the chicken coops each morning while I fill the feeders, gracing my hum-drum labour. One reason for the bird's population boom is that the female can incubate eggs while still feeding the fledglings of a previous clutch. Sometimes, however, this benefit of Nature can be overstretched; the squab on the lawn was malnourished. What to do with the body?

Some sentimental gesture made me launch it, arcing, into the air so it would fly once, at least. It landed in the ragwort patch, a pretty graveyard.

~

How many ways can one preserve tomatoes? So far I have puréed, sun-dried, bottled, frozen, ketchup, then hit upon chutney. My family are raising their eyes at purple beans at every dinner, but the glut of lettuce is easily solved; the way to a goose's stomach, and perhaps heart, is lettuce.

The kitchen is becoming a contested, congested area; having picked 5kg of figs – ripe, splitting, lubricious – from our tree, I have pots on every hob of the cooker simmering the fruit (along with rosemary, honey, red onions, red wine vinegar, red *pineau*) for chutney. Quite aside from the non-availability of cooking apparatus for others, the atmosphere is literally acid, and unbreathable. I decide to bottle in the great outdoors. In sterilized jars the chutney will keep for six months.

~

Zeb, my horse, died today. Yesterday evening, we went out for a meal at the bistro in Chefnay. When we came back, I took the two dogs for a walk up the track; a perfect evening of wine and rose sunshine and the long views. On the return, as we neared Zeb's small paddock to the front of the house, I saw him stagger. Madame Charlotte Monat, the vet, came, a night of hell ensued, him swirling on his side, intravenous drips by torchlight. At one stage, after being injected, he stood and rested his head on my shoulder. And I hoped, as you do.

About midday as the ketamine painkiller wore off, Zeb commenced wobbling again, and I asked Penny to phone Charlotte

Monat so he could be put down. His suffering was too much, for him, for me. As we waited, he keeled over into the fence – a heart attack. And there was no need for a vet. No need for any-one any more. At least I was there, to comfort him as he breathed his last. For his sake, not mine. Some days ago, I wrote an article about horses, and wanted to say that Zeb was my best mate, but felt embarrassed to do so. I wish I had. He was my best male friend. However, I do not wish to dwell on his death here, partly because writers are cursed by observing everything, including death, which they put into print, which is money, rendering trite and exploitative the deepest tragedies; and partly because humans are forever expounding on how Nature helps them: these days, all that matters is how we humans help Nature. I simply want it written somewhere Zeb was the finest horse that ever lived, because he deserves that memorial at least.

Our donkey Snowdrop, who loved him too, walks around in circles, and figures of eight. We pet her ten times a day, feed her an extra carrot, put her in with the sheep, so she has company. She walks around in circles, and figures of eight. Our poor donkey. Our poor donkey.

~

Waiting for SecAnim, the disposal company to come and col-lect Zeb's corpse for incineration, as dictated by French law. If it were up to me, I would bury him here at the house and weep and throw flowers over his grave. Daily. All I can do instead is have his picture as my PC screen saver. Modern life, eh?

In France, everything really does require paperwork and box-ticking: for the collection of Zeb, we have to confirm that the body of the horse is not near electricity cables, no reversing of the collec-tion lorry is required, and that the operator will not be required to remove any tarpaulin or other covering. Charlotte Monat, on giving us the requisite form at the veterinary surgery, shook her head with disbelief. Guillaume Roban, since he farms cattle, is well versed in animal disposal, and with his son moves Zeb's body, by strapping it to the front loader of their International tractor, to a suitable collection point beside the track. We are in the habit of giving Guillaume small gifts for his many kindnesses. 'Please don't give me anything this time,' he says. He also has a horse. He understands our sorrow. So do our neighbours, who offer condolences, and wish us 'Bon courage.' Zeb was a village favourite, the subject of many visits by parents with a kid in a buggy, or a toddler in hand. These are good people. This is a good place.

Three days we wait, Zeb's body mouldering under a tarpaulin (or a *bâche* as I have learned to call it; quite often the vocabulary that sticks is the vocabulary learned in adversity; I never forget the French for trailer, after our *remorque* lost a wheel on the A20 south of Brive-la-Gaillarde, leaving us with the interesting problem of how to get a rigid inflatable boat and an outboard motor in the car, plus the kids). Finally, the guy from SecAnim arrives – in usual French style, just half an hour's notice beforehand on the mobile – driving a massive open-backed lorry; I watch the lorry drive up the track, sending a cloud of chalk dust in its wake, past the sunflower fields, the sunflowers brown and burnt, ragged staggering survivors of a nuclear blast. The driver waves to us, smiles, drives into the paddock, operates the crane, and hoists Zeb's body up, and away, with a professionalism which gives us relief. No fuss. We give him the cheque for the disposal. Does he want to see Zeb's paperwork, equine passport? No. No fuss. And that is the difference between France and Britain. In France one frets about paperwork and rules which, in practice, *tout le monde* ignores;

in Britain, there is less paperwork, but in Britain the livestock disposal operative would have arrived, stroked his chin, and said, 'Oh, don't know, mate . . .' And extended our agony. This is the first day of autumn, a gold glint in the hedge, the gold filings of fallen leaves on the ground.

On the twenty-fourth we go to the farm show at Matha, and are shown to our parking by *jeunes agriculteurs* in orange-sun-gleaming hi-viz vests. In the festival field there is a display of tractors, old and new, then we walk along the stalls, with their local 'artisan' sausages, yogurt, honey, bric-a-brac, farm insurance companies. There is bale tossing, tractor riding, a display of poultry . . . so far, so familiar; it could be England. Then we encounter the producers of foie gras, snail terrine, tins of snails, snail sausages. This could only be rural France. Polite, epicurean, elemental.

Dinner in the evening (nineteen euros for adults, including drinks) is *repas terroir*, a celebration of local produce:

Apéritif local
Melon d'Authon-Ébéon
Jambon de pays et Pineau des Charentes
Jambon à la broche de Vibrac et mojhette de
Pont l'Abbé d'Arnoult
Coup du milieu de Matha
Assiette salade d'Aumagne et fromages des
Charentes et du Poitou
Galette charentaise
Yaourt de Pamplie
Café

Apart from the coffee the ingredients come from within a twenty kilometres radius, and are produced by small-scale farmers. Big Farmer and the industrialization of agriculture may win the globe in the end, but France will be the last country to fall. In France, the fierce appreciation of food means that people will support its production. Pay a fair price. Walk the extra kilometre to an *épicerie*, or a street stall. Drive to a young couple supplying their dreamy goat's cheese from a farm barn in Villejésus.

There was, it almost goes without saying, no vegetarian option in the *repas terroir*. I have never seen one at a dinner in France, private or public, where the automatic assumption is universal carnivorism. When the city of Lyon put a vegetarian option on the school lunch menu the government accused the city authorities of 'unacceptable insult' to France's farmers and butchers. *Sud Ouest*'s headline was: 'Menu sans viande; un risque pour la santé?'

AUTUMN

SEPTEMBER

In the wheat field behind the house, the post-harvest hush, and the sense of summer ending. On a strand of sagging barbed wire on the track to the wood a single yellowhammer drones, 'A-little-bit-of-bread-and-no-cheese.A-little-bit-of-bread-and-no-cheese.' Everywhere, the incipient melancholy of September. Everywhere summer is dying, except beside the stream, that is. Nature does not work to a uniform, all-enveloping timescale. By the stream in La Roche, there is no such stillness, no such sense of summer being over. September is the stream's lush time. Along the banks, the flowers bloom.

It has been a long, hot afternoon (helping a neighbour with the combining, breathless work on a breathless day) and I've come down to the stream for a swim; and I suppose a dose of invigoration. A swim in a time and place like this is a recapturing, albeit temporary, of the vitality of spring and early summer. When the views were all forwards.

Perhaps 'swim' is over-description; the stream, at best, widens and deepens into a grey stone basin three strokes long, three feet deep – a plunge pool made by Nature. It used to be the old *lavoir*, where the women of the village did the washing. Entering, I wade up to my knees, sending two trout scuttling into the shadowed water under the alders. And then I launch myself, the arms of the delirious cold water behind my back, the prow of my chin creating tiny bow waves. The scent of the water is wild and green. The dog joins me, swimming long, ottery-backed circles, before heading to a bed of sunlight on shingle, and sprawling instantly asleep, in that worry-free way Labradors possess.

I stay in the water, playing 'boats', doing nothing on the downstream laps, merely letting the slow current carry me past the water mint. The plant has a slumberous smell, to help the mind drift away.

~

Technically, one harvests when the grapes are 'physiologically ripe', firm and sweet. Easy to write, less easy to determine in practice, when you have several different varieties, in two different locations. And grey mould. The thirty vines, some of them very young, took only hours to pick – or rather, cut with secateurs – then depose the bunches in the wheelbarrow, then tip the two loads down the purpose-built shaft into the *cave*, and the pressing room. By the time I'd sorted out the rotten and the underripe, I had 20lbs of fruit. Enough for a mere thirty bottles of wine.

For a mad moment in the historic twilight of the pressing room I am tempted to crush the clusters of grapes peasant-style, by treading on them barefoot, but realize I would never then drink the result. Instead, I put the clusters through a mechanical crusher on top of the Vigo fruit press, an old mechanical friend. (We used it in Herefordshire for pressing apples.) I leave the crushed 'must' for a day; red wine is left in contact with its skins to garner colour, flavour, whereas white wine is allowed very little skin contact. And I want the wild yeasts of the air for fermentation, rather than introducing a strain of yeast. The juice flows out of the Vigo press, golden in the shafts of light through the *cave* windows.

I had wanted to restore the wooden wine-press in the *cave*, but never found the time, because there never is enough time. I had wanted, also, to use the stone fermentation vat, but thirty bottles' worth is barely above the outlet pipe, so instead fermentation occurs in stainless steel buckets. There is still 'clarification' – the racking from one vessel to another in the hope of leaving the solids ('pomace') behind in the bottom of the fermentation tank – to go. To help precipitate dead yeast cells to the bottom of the buckets, I add egg whites, as advised by Madame Roban.

Quite an involved process, winemaking.

~

A painted lady butterfly on my finger as I type this, front window of the study open; the butterfly leaves at its own discretion, not at my indication. The lime tree's fruits, like peppercorns on pale wings, spin and sail in the wind. Lingering flies on lingering blackberries, and the trees along the track heaped with wild clematis. Under each lime tree, a bicycle: again, magazine-photograph France. I am calculating my yield per square metre of the *potager*; roughly, this is three times the amount per square metre compared to my previous large-scale farming. So, proof of Nobel-prize-winner Amartya Sen's observation that, contrary to the claims of Big Farmer, yield is inverse to area in farming, due to the greater care the farmer is able to extend to small areas. Small is not only beautiful, it is productive.

I have become mildly obsessed with chicory; partly because the paddock in which Zeb died was bright with its blue flower (it has thus become my own personal flower of mourning), and partly because it so accurately forecasts the weather. When I was very young my grandmother, a farmer's spouse, took me for toddles along the deep and winding lanes of east Herefordshire, to suddenly announce under the clear blue sky, 'It's going to rain.' And we would scurry home, beating the rain plops, and have victorious Rich Tea biscuits beside the Rayburn Royal. Grandma's own personal meteorologist was not Mr Fish of the Met Office, but a commonplace wildflower, scarlet pimpernel. *Anagallis arvensis*, she insisted, closed its bright red head when rain was approaching.

So indispensable was the scarlet pimpernel to the weather-watchers of yore that its common names were, along with 'shepherd's weatherglass', the 'poor man's weatherglass' and 'ploughman's weatherglass'. But many other native wildflowers, as many as thirty, share the gift of weather-prediction, among them bindweed, dandelion, daisy, germander speedwell, red campion, and wood sorrel, common chickweed, white stitchwort, wood anemone, purple sandwort and wild chicory. Before moving to France, wild chicory was largely unknown to me, but having spent hours with the flower, in *potager* and paddock, I can confirm it is an especially sensitive petal, shutting hours before rain, reopening hours before the good weather times return.

My peasant life in France: I now forecast the weather by the flowers.

~

Under a plank in the paddock a mass of cagouillards, the small and grey (hence 'le petit-gris') snail regarded as the star of 'gastronomie charentaise'. I find myself un-tempted.

~

Our sunflower patch down by the barely trickling brook is ripe for the harvesting; the brown leaves are poppadom-snappy. Guillaume Roban has offered to cut the lot with his combine (there is just enough room to get the Claas combine into the field, and a single run would do the job) but authenticity, perhaps pride, requires me to do the job myself. With the Husqvarna 522HDR60X petrol hedge cutter.

Was it too much *Bill and Ben* on TV as a child? Cutting off the sunflowers at knee height seems a cruelty until, with my back breaking, I flip into endurance mode, and I raze the six-feet-high flowers without hesitation. Swallows fly overhead, and one dips down from the sky to take a sip from the pond by the brook, a sort of salutation before it goes south for its summer. I would like to think that he or she was from the *hirondelle* broods raised in our barn. A solipsism, an arrogance, a fancy. Or perhaps not. Perhaps in some unfathomable way, the birds know their friends.

A couple of days back I went into the barn, and on the nails of a rear rafter, where someone had once hung tools, sat juvenile *hirondelles*, one to each nail. I said, 'Désolé,' and apologized for disturbing their roosting.

Meanwhile, the eighth-of-an-acre plot of sunflowers resembles the scene of a human massacre. But overlaid with the scent of ginger cake. Then I think, 'Today I, for the first time in my life, cut sunflowers.' And, from the *oubliette* of memory, a conversation by the banks of the Dordogne, fifteen years ago. Driving back from holiday in Spain (a mere thousand miles . . . an outboard motor in the boot) we stopped at a farm in Vitrac which did overnight camping. The farmer, Philippe Masson, and I got to talking about our respective farms. Mine in west Herefordshire was too wet. His was too dry . . . the usual farmers' laments. After an hour of bantering 'onedownsman-ship' he suggested that my family should try farming in France. We did. Eventually. Sometimes dreams come true.

~

Sitting outside the *bar-tabac* in Chefnay at a classic round metal table: me with my *noisette*, Penny with her *grand crème* reading *Sud Ouest* – for which 'regional newspaper' does no justice at all to its circulation, intellectual editorials, breadth of interest, precis of national and international news, microscopic focus on the very local. Usefully, the back sports pages, featuring the pre-season news about Stade Rochelais, are in my face. I like rugby, played in the first XV at school, listened on a handheld transistor radio in the Land Rover when Jonny Wilkinson 'in the pocket' won the 2003 Rugby World Cup, but my reading about La Rochelle's stellar team is, if honest, 50 per cent about assimilation. When conversation with French friends floun-ders, I say 'Stade Rochelais'; there is an eruption of breaking ice regardless of gender.

From inside the *bar-tabac* comes the smell of garlic, frying butter, vinegar cleaning liquid: the odours of provincial France.

~

High in an apple tree in the small orchard. Orbs of fruit hang-ing around my head; a private constellation of red planets. Where the sun touches through the leaves the apples become encircled with goldshine.

The day did not begin like this. In the early morning there was the sort of mist which is actually fog and it had a choke-hold on the valley. I could barely breathe, and when I was at the top of the ladder picking the apples – Reine des Reinettes, a nineteenth-century French heritage breed, 'King of the Pippins' – my head was in a blind bag.

But the sun of summer came back for a last, valiant hurrah. September sunlight is hazy and imprecise, and cannot be mistaken for the sunlight of any other month. But it banished the fog, except down in the village. I can see the mist down there now, severing the square tower of the twelfth-century *église*, so it is sandcastle proportioned. The two Charente departments are snow-scattered with Romanesque churches; there are four within a four-kilometre radius, each as beautifully adorned with carvings and gargoyles as the other.

Down the aluminium ladder I go, for the umpteenth time, to unload the nylon McKinley haversack – attached to my front – containing the plucked fruit. Each apple is methodically placed in a wooden box; these are the apples for storage, for family eating on winter nights by the fire.

The haversack is adequate as picking pouch; when I was a child doing this exact same job I had a brown canvas satchel, which my persuasive father charmed off the shoulder of the postman. The satchel had GPO stamped on the side. I wish I still had the satchel; it was the best of picking pouches.

I move the ladder to the other side of the tree; climb back, breathily. A tree creeper in the adjoining row of trees saunters up the trunk with cheery, juxtaposed ease.

In the damson, a chiffchaff is calling; the bird's speech is more wistful on its September departure than on its March arrival. Then there are the clamorous chickens beneath me. I drop any irredeemably maggoty fruit, the apples with shrivelled faces, for them. They know this.

Nature's Law is Sod's Law. Consequently, the perfect, pulchritudinous fruit is always beyond convenient reach, forever situated on the absolute edge of my Heavens, requiring me to get off the ladder, and clamber along branches.

High in an apple tree, the normal rules of life are suspended. (Reality only occurs when you are sitting under an apple tree, and an apple lands on your head.) There is something deliciously childish in climbing an apple tree. Something quietly thought-provoking too; because up in a tree one has reversed evolution. Become an ape-man.

Up here in my dreamy apple tree, listening to the chiffchaff, I can believe those anthropologists who claim that the ape-men sang like birds before they learned to talk. I want to sing like a bird up here.

I don't wear gloves: the feel of an apple in the hand is the perfect means of judging perfect ripeness. Also, there is the pleasure of it, the power of it. An apple in the hand is more satisfying, more potent than any other fruit.

Gloves, of course, would save my hands from wasp stings. In the Garden of Eden, the snake was the Devil's instrument. In a fruit orchard, Lucifer assumes the winged shape of *Vespula vulgaris*. For much of their life wasps are carnivores, but in September they madden for sappy apples. They drone constantly around me, rivalrous, and I am waiting for the first sting, which will also be, like the smothering mist, a bite of winter.

I have hand-picked all I can from this venerable Reine des Reinettes, so I return to Earth to shake down the tree, using a shepherd's crook gaffer-taped to a long hazel pole.

I start shaking the tree. The apples storm down. Giant red hail stones. Little fruit comets. The chickens flee, fluttery and feathery.

This shaken-down fruit will become cider vinegar for,

among other dishes, my pickled eggs infused with herbs. Cider made by me, eggs from our chickens, herbs from my own plots, fertilized with manure from said fowl.

Self-sufficiency, you could say. Or *autarcie*, if you were French. Circles of Heaven and Earth certainly.

~

Tonight, I walk with the dogs to the very top of the escarpment. From the west a wind has come.

There is only me, and the dogs. The wind bats the leaves off the oaks; the leaves, thin and starved, swirl around us. The philosopher Albert Camus declared autumn a 'second spring', where 'every leaf is a flower'. A French fancy. Today the leaves are brown, just brown. As the dogs and I stand there in the thumping wind a hen harrier hunts low over the pokey stubble of Guillaume's fifty-acre sunflower field. The bird is a small grey cloud. She comes towards us, deliberate and slow.

She is almost on us, before she veers up overhead. Then I see that she was towing on her tail a black squall. In a matter of seconds the rain devours the view, all twenty open miles of it.

We head for home. On the way back down, the water coursing along the limestone track, ferrying leaves and sticks, we met Guillaume Roban walking the other way, en route to check his cows. From under the hood of his khaki cagoule he gives me an arch smile: 'Le temps anglais.'

Vraiment. We try further conversation but it is useless. The wind keeps taking our words away, along with the leaves.

So, autumn.

OCTOBER

I went up into the woods today. There were surprises, but none involving teddy bears and picnicking.

I went alone, because you go to the woods for solitude, not companionship. No one comes looking for you in a wood for an opinion, an answer, a signature, a form requiring ticking.

I say alone, but I had a dog. The dog in question, the Border terrier, is a case of canine nominative determinism. My son, Tris, named him Rupert, Army slang for an officer, when he was a six-week-old puppy. And Rupert really has become quite bossy. He likes to check that all is pukka on his parade ground which, as far as I can determine, is the entire world. On a walk the only way to prevent him endlessly stopping and sniffing is to quick-march.

The dog has put on weight, making him a portly canine colonel. Consequently, he is on an exercise regime. Me too, but for the healing of my ruptured knee ligaments; they had got better, but then I did something stupid . . . So, more *bougez!* Walking semi-cured the malady last time, so it is walking again for at least three kilometres a day.

And in honesty, I needed escape. I'd spent the entire morning packing dried leaves and flowers of wild marjoram and bay trees – both of which grow as providential weed on our warm, limestone land, and are joyously oblivious to days upon days of biblical drought – only to realize that the electronic scales were errantly calibrated, and the job required redoing, including the retying of the exquisite deep mauve bows (the colour of marjoram flowers) and green bows (the colour of *Laurus nobilis*) at the top of each packet. It is not all macho tractor-driving glory, farming, especially the peasant end.

So, the dog and I set off up the track beside the Robans' harvested sunflower field at a furious pace, the mood to match.

In open French countryside on a shimmering October afternoon one can persuade oneself it is still summer.

When we entered the shadow of the wood, no such deceit was plausible. The shadow of the wood was the shadow of winter approaching.

There are woods that straggle gently into being. Not so the Bois des Chaumes, which sits astride our hilltop like a walled citadel, entered through a portcullis.

Birdsong was minimal. From behind a drape of old man's beard, a jay shrieked imprecations. Two blackbirds 'chinked' at each other: and I was never so aware that birdsong is conversation. And I was excluded.

For mile after mile the trees remained irrevocably insentient. In October one becomes aware of the withdrawal into self that is the truth of the autumnal process of the arboreal life form. The leaves of the dogwood were turning red, an incontrovertible sign of the coming of autumn in chalkland.

The white track we followed appeared endless, because the wood melds into others to form a vast Charentais forest. The labour required to make the *chemin* must have been fantastic, taking many hands many years.

The dog strained at his leash to investigate a savaged wood ants' nest; the tumpy nest glistened black with gangs of ants making repairs. Their slave work too was fantastic.

We pounded up a rise; from the top of the pitch, the view was long and narrow; a gorge through close-pressing trees, behind which were piles of old timber stacked up like shipwrecks.

So we ran for it and, as we ran faster and faster, the track opened up like a bloom. I was whooping, he was barking; because in the middle of a French forest there is no one to hear you scream with joy. An extraordinary thing, in the twenty-first century, to be absolutely alone; original; Adam.

At the bottom, panting, I swigged from my *gourde*, my reusable water bottle; the dog lapped water out of my scooped hand. From a bramble bush I crushed some blackberries into the bottle to make a fruit juice.

Something about those childish capers, the running and the faux-Ribena, altered the mood of the day. The healing power of Nature is famed; less well known is Nature's tendency to amplify one's existing mood. Like alcohol.

Simultaneously, the dog and I both thought, the hell with it. Henceforth, we would wood-wander at a pace of our making, and we did. I did the stopping and sniffing, he did the leading, in any direction he wanted.

Thus it was, we entered upon the deer track, a thin line of cracked mud which transported us deep into a region of grassy glades, pools of sunlight, splashes of shade, streams of clear breeze. Gatekeeper butterflies fountained from the wild marjoram and ragwort.

The deer track fed into a forgotten cartway, waist high with grass. Around the sixth or seventh bend we came upon a wooden sign, hanging skew-whiff on the side of an oak announcing, 'Le Verger'. The orchard.

On the sign someone had carved, in addition to the necessary nomenclatura of possession, two hearts and two flowers. There were eight gnarly walnut trees, the lot of them bowed with green globes of crop. The greater surprise, though, of the secret orchard, long abandoned, were the red deer hinds dozing beneath the trees' secluding shade.

I have never been so close to hinds. Until that hour I had never understood why St Hubert was turned from a callous, big-bag hunter into a holy man, respectful of God's creatures, after a forest encounter with a deer. But at the secret orchard I too had a revelation.

I have never shot a deer and I knew then that I never will. The Normans had their Beasts of Venery, the noble animals worth hunting. I have developed in mid-life an anti-Venery, a personal list of the game too beautiful to kill. So red deer join teal, and hares. A sentimental feeling for beauty seems a consequence of age.

It makes no sense – I will continue to occasionally shoot pigeons and rabbits for the pot – but we are our inconsistencies.

Whatever: the dog and I, unwilling to break the dream of deer in the secret orchard, withdrew, and wended our way home. For a few hours we had, in one way or another, held at bay the autumn of our years.

Wonderful too, we both thought, to see deer so close.

~

That night, we had the first log fire since March. It was not cold (it doesn't really get cold in the Charente until January) but I wanted to protest against the dwindling of the light. The dogs took up position in front of the flames, which is as it should be, always has been. Out in the darkness, the first trotter prints of wild boar were filling with rain. We went out for *apéros* with friends, and came home late; as the car headlights sprayed the verge by the village sign they illuminated a male wild boar – glistening and tusky. It looked like something from a cave painting.

~

If harvesting sunflower was a first, my harvesting of my hops is a perfumed blast from the past. It is an idyllic Charente morning when I pull away the bines, and sever them with a knife. If the vines were a failure, the hops have been a success; the wall of the courtyard has protected them from the south sun, while their exposure to the north wind has allowed plenty of anti-pestilential air through the plants. As I work, the ivy flowers on the hay barn are worked by hummingbird hawk-moths.

To dry the cones – still attached to the bines – I heap them along a ten-metre length of cord tied between two fruit trees in the front garden; they look like a line of green lawyers' wigs.

I have a dream of one day making my own beer, and bittering it with my own home-grown hops, but these cones, drying in the Charente sun, will be bagged for potpourri or put in small cotton bags as pillows to aid sleep. A while ago I mentioned to a relative in Herefordshire that I'd grown hops, and she said, 'I'd love some dried.' She told someone else, who told someone else, and the chain-whisper went on and on. We are going back to Britain for a weekend before Christmas, to visit relatives and friends. The 'order book' for my herbs, posh pickled eggs, *vin de noix* and hops – the latter being the ultimate in 'coals to Newcastle' – is already too much for the boot and back seat of our autoroute-eating German estate. So we are now going there in the Citroën Berlingo. Very slowly.

~

My study is decked with hops above the fireplace. I asked both children, expecting a no, whether they too would like to deck their rooms with hops. Both said yes, and the house from top to bottom is perfumed.

This morning I bumped into our least welcome, though most mesmerizing, house guest: a scutigerid, a bristly centipede. The creature was in the hall, scuttling around, limited in eyesight, unnervingly fast on its (many) legs. I gingerly trapped it with a wine glass, and threw it out of the door.

If we ever hear a guest screaming in the shower, I think, 'Scutigerid.' I confess to emitting a distinct 'Aarrgh' myself last year on the subject of creepy crawlies; I turned on the bedside light to see an Expressionist shadow of a crouching vampire. The reality was, shall we say, interesting: a four-inch-long, lime-green praying mantis was sitting on the headboard, looking down at me.

~

4 October. Fig picking, again. But the wet of the last two days has swollen half the crop, which have split apart, to display their fleshy, moist insides; red admiral butterflies and bees are enjoying the crop of their lives. Making fig chutney again.

~

5 October. No rain, and the wind, bless it now, is bringing down the walnuts. Up the hill, the clinky din of harrowing, the spurting flight of finches, the trackside hedge rattling with sparrows, the whirl and whistle of a thousand starlings in the wheat stubble.

The sound of the evening in autumn: Guillaume Roban taking cut maize in the link box of the Fiat tractor to the cows, who bellock at his approach, just as the bells of La Roche bell. Overhead, the chatter of redwings, migrants from the north; I

like redwings, and I like too the way the pristine wilderness of
the Far North trails on their wing-beats. But redwings are the
cold darts of winter in any hope of warmth here and now, in
the hope of a lingering summer. In the clarity and dryness of
the Charente air there is no mediating moisture, so the wind is
always razor-backed. By lamplight in the cellar, I rack and bottle fifteen bottles of wine.

Again, the next morning I open the shutters to an icy sky,
blue and blinding. A brave common blue butterfly flutters
around me – a tumbled mosaic tile from the lapis lazuli dome
above. In the orchard, a host of redwings are pillaging the
rowan trees, the birds' mouths an untidy scarlet from the gorging on the bloody berries.

Something about the redwings' rapaciousness, their focused
intent, makes me dress and get out early to forage. My mission
this morning is collecting sloes. Make hay while the sun shines
is the farmer's maxim; pick hedgerow berries when Jack Frost
visits is the forager's. Frost on autumn fruit, it softens and it
sweetens.

Sloes, the fruits of the blackthorn, are the wild great-
grandparents of the damson; only the purple colour of the skin
suggests the genetic connection – the damson is sweet; the Day-
Glo-green flesh of the sloe, when bitten into, makes the mouth
wafer-dry. If frost sweetens the sloes, further alchemy, in kitchen and cellar, is still required for most human tastes.

All hedgerow fruits possess a design of temptation; rosehips
proffer themselves on the end of bare wires, blaring red lights,
and viewable for country miles; purple elderberries hang in
luscious chandeliers; sloes cluster their twigs, juicy mass in
small space. This is a good year for sloes locally, and I dream
during my work of the country Christmas treats of sloe gin,

game sauce, sloe jelly, and my *pièce de résistance*, chocolate sloes.

But Nature's motto for humans is: 'No gain without pain.' The globose sloes are protected by two-inch woody spikes. I've tried picking with leather gloves, but they are clumsy, so I am back to bare hands; the black thorns have made scarlet berries of my blood. But is this a bad thing, to experience Nature red in thorn? Observing Nature really only makes use of the senses of sight, hearing and smell. Do we not miss something if our fingers have never felt the sealing-wax smoothness of the rosehip, suffered the scratch of the bramble, or rubbed the dull dust of yeast from a sloe's skin to reveal the intense, lustrous purple below? And are we not actually closest to Nature, value it most, when we pick it? When we are inside the food chain ourselves?

Such is my menu of thought, this October morning when the sky is blue and blinding, the redwings are gorging. And the sloes are as big as grapes.

Chocolate Sloes (Prunelles au Chocolat)

The English country person's chocolate liqueurs, with a French twist, namely cognac instead of gin.

8oz 70% dark chocolate (ideally organic, ethical)
6oz cognac-soaked sloes
1 level dessertspoon of wildflower honey
pinch of Île de Ré hand-harvested salt
rice paper

Melt the chocolate. Chop the flesh off the sloes, and add to the melted chocolate. Stir in the honey and salt. Let the confection set on the rice paper, then cut into squares. *Voilà!*

I read the birds, like a priest of Ancient Rome. On Monday a party of fieldfares came skimming south, just under the stars.

The gale was on their wings. For two days the wind went over us like the teeth of a saw. Then it collapsed, exhausted, leaving yesterday's evening sun-sore-red.

So, the signs were indeed auspicious (from Latin *auspex*, meaning, loosely, 'to look at the flight of birds'), and augured well (from Latin *augur*, the diviner who foretold events from the behaviour of birds). Sure enough, when I went into the orchard this morning, the gale had brought all the walnuts down. Green, split-skinned globes lay around in their masses under the trees and in the five grass alleyways between the trees' parade-straight lines.

The autumn sky was impossibly blue.

There are two ways to begin the walnut harvest. You shake the tree mechanically to loosen the ripe nuts. Or you hope and wait for the wind to do the job for you, and have the wind followed by a dry day for the picking. This year the gods and their elements are on my side.

The agricultural delivery company is not. The clever, sit-on petrol-powered picking machine I was intending to rent is delayed, so I am obliged to use a *rouleau ramasse noix* borrowed from Madame Giraud. The *rouleau* can only be described as a wire-mesh rugby ball on the end of a long handle. You roll the 'rugby ball' over the nuts, and when the ball is full it is emptied into a plastic crate. The action is like hoovering with an old-fashioned Ewbank carpet cleaner. It does at least save bending over.

Anyway, getting the *rouleau* out from Madame Giraud's shed I experienced all the usual feelings about starting a harvest. The not unnatural relief at commencement, the hope of success and plenty.

After two hours' work: a sense of panic about the enormity of the task.

Our orchard is a third of an acre; then I have the lanes of the village, and Madame Giraud's five-acre rented orchard, though one acre is a spiky sea of dogwood, bramble and buddleia scrub, from which the walnut trees, all of them about twenty years of age, emerge like dingy masts under sail. The walnuts there we picked 'green' off the trees in July, for pickling and *vin de noix*. We leave the scrub to keep the hares and nightingales.

Toil, like grief, exists in discrete stages. After pleasure and panic comes acceptance, then a sort of Zen contentment. Even the occasional clogging of the *rouleau* from the walnut casings fails to break this mood.

Every type of farmland has its peculiar aroma. The whiff of walnut orchards is that of school disinfectant from the lab's worth of chemicals in the nut's husk, predominantly juglone. (5-Hydroxy-1,4-naphthoquinone is a natural toxin, which acts as a protective herbicide and pesticide for the trees; historically humans have used juglone as a tanning agent in hair and leather dyes. By the same token, handling the immature nuts causes black hand syndrome.)

Then: through a gap in the hedge, between the cascades of wild clematis with their Scottie-dog whiskers, old Monsieur Roban starts ploughing the hundred-acre field, the stones clinking against the metal blades.

The church bell tings the half-hours. The *rouleau* clickety-clacks, clickety-clacks.

A red admiral butterfly circles me cautiously. *Vanessa atalanta*, as well as having the loveliest of Latin names, is the cleverest of the order Lepidoptera; the butterfly 'habituates' or learns to react to stimuli. The red admiral is assessing my capacity for harm.

Contrary to received wisdom, the 'admiral' in the butterfly's name is not a corruption of 'admirable', but a recognition that its wing patches resemble the flags of a Royal Navy admiral in the seventeenth century.

Starlings fall in a meteor shower on the turned earth from Monsieur Roban's plough. At the top of the orchard I discover my own disrupted ground, as if an artillery shell had exploded; the wild boar have snout-ploughed the sward here, seeking wild carrot tubers.

Bees make beelines of flight; butterflies have the movement pattern of absent-minded aunts around a sitting room.

Since the trees are young, there is open sky between the rows. Up in the blue dome swallows are chattering and massing. Their swirl gets steadily thicker, as others join.

A walnut harvest would be incomplete without the occasional sampling of the product. After pulling off the green outer husk, I roll a walnut under my wellingtoned foot, so that the familiar pitted wooden shell opens at the seams, then I carefully prise the halves apart to extract the kernel whole. It is the shape and form of a human brain. But albino.

The kernel, to my small disappointment, is smaller than those from the memory of Christmases past. A consequence, I suppose, of neglect. The orchard has been untended for years, and is in need of that indispensable arboreal booster: chicken shit.

Before their weeks and months of traditional drying (ours go into the hayloft), walnuts have a hint of bitterness in the aftertaste. I rather like it. I like too the health benefits of walnuts, the antioxidants and the omegas. Seven walnuts a day is said to keep the doctor away.

Through the gap in the hedge, on the horizon, an unknown man walks with intent towards the wood, his pointer dog before him. The sun flashes on the barrel of his rifle, slung over his shoulder. The antiquity of such a scene brings to mind that passage in Spanish philosopher José Ortega y Gasset's *Meditations on Hunting*, the world's classic on the subject and published in French as *Sur la chasse*:

> 'Natural' man is always there, under the changeable historical man. We call him and he comes – a little sleepy, benumbed, without his lost form of instinctive hunter, but, after all, still alive. Natural man is first prehistoric man – the hunter.

Harvesting nuts is also an atavistic state. Natural man is gatherer as well as hunter.

At about eleven, with some 50kg of nuts collected, I suddenly look up. The air above me is silent. The swallows have gone, as though they had never existed.

But again: the impossible blue of the sky.

French Walnut Cake

Serves 8

200g butter
250g caster sugar
300g ground walnuts
70g flour
4 eggs
finely grated zest of 1 unwaxed lemon

30ml rum
a dozen half-walnuts

Preheat the oven to 150°C/300°F and line a 20cm/8inch round tin on the base and sides.

Beat the butter and sugar until the mixture turns white. Mix in the ground walnuts, flour, eggs, lemon zest and rum, and stir vigorously. Fill buttered tin with the mixture and bake for about an hour.

When done, allow to cool at room temperature and then turn the cake out of the tin and place the half-walnuts on top as decoration.

Sweet Honey Walnuts

1 unwaxed lemon
500g clear honey (single flower)
2–3 cloves
1 cinnamon stick
400g walnut kernels
salt
2 sprigs fresh thyme

Pare the rind from the lemon with a zester, and juice the lemon. Put 500ml of water in a large pan. Add the honey, cloves, cinnamon, lemon juice and rind. Bring to the boil, then reduce the heat and simmer gently for fifteen minutes, while stirring, until thick and syrupy. Remove from heat.

Meanwhile, bring a pan of salted water to the boil. Add the walnuts and cook for five minutes; then strain and leave the walnuts to dry. Add the walnuts and thyme to the honey syrup. Heat gently, stirring until boiling.

Transfer the walnuts to three 500g/18fl oz Kilner jars that have been thoroughly washed. Pour over the remaining syrup to cover the walnuts and leave to cool. Seal and leave to marinate in a cool dark place for one week. The walnuts will keep for about five months.

On average, the French eat 500g of walnuts per capita every year, or in other terms, everyone in France eats a walnut a week, all year round. Thus I have no problem at all bartering 400kg of walnuts. For fowl, and flesh, and honey from other local producers; the young couple with the goats and Rouen ducks over at Villejésus, Jean-Paul at Haimps with his Maraîchine cattle, and the Phillipots at the garage, who have thirty hives behind the repair workshop. (And close down the car business for two weeks a year to tend the bees and collect the honey.)

~

Morning, late October. Our two dogs, the puppyish female black Labrador, Plum, and stately male Border terrier, Rupert, start barking uncontrollably at something beyond the stone wall of the front garden.

The usual cause of such canine commotion is the escape of the donkey. So I grab a lead rope, march outside and open the wooden front gate – but instead of Snowdrop there is a bedraggled and aged golden Labrador. Her eyelid is cut; her eyes welling with despair.

I look up and down the track for her owner. Nobody. My stomach sinks.

The French have the bad habit of dumping dogs. Indeed, they top the European league table for abandoned canines – at a rate of sixty thousand a year (compared to sixteen thousand in the UK). This is a country in which the state is so omnipresent and munificent, people are aghast at the thought of paying for anything other than themselves. So out the door goes Fido. But perhaps this dog has wandered up from the village?

I give her a tickle under the chin, fetch her a bowl of water, which she laps greedily. I shut the gate.

Fifteen minutes later, I go to check that she's gone home.

But she is still by the gate. Still looking tired, still hungry. So I invite her in.

She hobbles over the threshold and into our garden. As well as being exhausted, she is suffering from arthritis, and is fat as a buttered croissant. Her claws rival an eagle's talons.

She comes in, sits, raises her paw. I know Labradors are genetically engineered to play on human emotions, but this is unbearable. Surely no one could have abandoned such a lovely, gentle dog?

She wolfs down a bowl of dog food. A family conference ensues.

First, Penny does the obvious thing. She phones Jean-Luc, one of the village's unofficial elders, and a Labrador owner himself, to see if he knows of a missing dog.

Non.

So, next we put the dog in the back of the car, and take her to Charlotte Monat in Chefnay. After all, French dogs aged over four months are required by law to be identified by a microchip or tattoo.

Also, all French dogs are obliged to be registered with the Ministry of Agriculture and Forests, and have to possess an ID card, a 'Carte d'Identification de Mon Animal'.

At the veterinary surgery Charlotte Monat is opening the double doors to usher out an elderly couple carrying a blood-hound with a row of criss-cross stitches down its leg.

'Nous avons trouvé cette chienne . . .' I say, signalling to the boot. Madame Monat's lips tighten into a grimace of resignation and she goes off to fetch the microchip scanner.

The elderly couple are retired Germans, living locally. Their dog had been abandoned, too, but on a roadside. 'You have to do something for these dogs,' the woman says, pointing at the two pathetic animals sitting in car boots.

Madame Monat scans for microchips, checks for ID tattoos. Nothing. She gives a Gallic shrug of despair.

'Her health?' I ask. Again, the Gallic shrug. 'The back legs, obviously ... The eye cut is nothing.'

By law, abandoned or lost dogs must be reported to the local *mairies*. We agree with Madame Monat to divide out the notifications between us.

But then came the elephant in the room, or rather the portly Labrador in the car park. Who would look after the dog while it was determined whether an owner would come forward or be located?

'White Dog' – as the family were starting to call her – could go to the local pound. But how nice would that be for her, hurt and bewildered?

'Nous la gardons,' I suddenly said to Madam Monat. We will keep her.

A fateful moment. Freda has a love of looking after animal waifs and strays, which never seem to leave. As a child she used to give her Christmas present money to the Dogs Trust charity, and slept with her miniature Jack Russell, Snoopy, under her bed. Even today she tells everybody, 'I grew up in a family of eight: four humans and four dogs.'

On the way home, we stop by the town pharmacy to buy dog wormer and flea treatment. (Every small French town has a pharmacy, a bank, an insurance office, a motoring school and three *coiffeuses*.) 'Forty-four euros!' I lament in my grumpy father voice.

White Dog sits in the boot, happily looking out of the window.

Back home, in the afternoon rain, I walk off with a photo of White Dog to ask Guillaume if he can identify her. From the vantage point of his tractor cab he sees and knows everything.

As it happens, he is coming the other way along the track, hidden beneath his green plastic cape, on his way to check the cattle.

'We found . . .' I begin in French, showing him the limp A4 photograph.

'Yes, I saw her in your courtyard,' he replies. 'I also saw a car in the forest in the morning. 75 plates.'

Paris plates. Says it all. This was also not the first time dogs have been dumped in the forest – last summer holidays a black Labrador came along the track, frothing at the mouth, thin and too traumatized to accept our offers of help, beyond a few thrown biscuits.

Back at the house, further difficulties were beginning. Perhaps White Dog was abandoned because she was sick?

I guess her age to be around twelve. 'Think this might be palliative care,' I whisper to Penny.

But, if it were the end, we would make it a wonderful last few days or weeks for White Dog. In case she was harbouring an infectious disease, we decide to quarantine her for forty-eight hours in the grassy courtyard, with its cosy stone shed, away from Plum and Rupert.

However, she staunchly refuses to go into the shed, despite plenty of food and a bounty of blankets piled a foot deep. She only wants to sit by the back door.

So Freda and I build her a temporary kennel from wood and tarpaulin to keep her warm, and eventually, after two days, we manage to entice her into the house.

On entry, she immediately pees all over the stone kitchen

floor. A rescue dog, I realize, is not a blank slate: White Dog's brain was imprinted with her past. And it does not take Sherlock Holmes to deduce she has probably been kept all her life in a yard – she had no conception of 'inside' etiquette.

She hardly seems domesticated at all. As soon as any shopping is put down, she seizes the baguette. And once she has eaten her bowl of food she raids the bins. And, scoping our chickens, she drools and proceeds to give keen, if lumbering, chase.

I was never expecting our new canine companion to understand English, but it soon transpires she does not even comprehend French, or indeed universal dog-sign language, such as palm flat in face for 'stop'. She is partly deaf. She is completely untutored. She flinches if we go to stroke her. She has been abused.

But can you teach an old dog new tricks?

Yes, we discover, with kindness . . . and with tiny bits of Emmental cheese as a reward. And after four days, she goes outside to pee.

She is very patient with us. Inspirationally so. Throughout everything, she looks at us with what seems to be a smile on her face. Freda shampoos her, takes her for walks, cuts her claws. White Dog laps it all up.

In France, any dog unclaimed after eight days is to be rehomed – or put down (about fifty thousand unwanted dogs and cats are euthanized annually in the Hexagon). It is a rule.

Eight days pass . . . and nobody comes for White Dog. And I am glad they do not.

~

My daily cycle into Chefnay for the newspaper, usually twenty minutes each way, is taking more than an hour or two. I cycle over walnuts; the road, lined by mature walnut trees, is tar-macked by black husks. On the return leg, I am unable to resist filling a backpack, and two carrier bags, one hung off each handle bar. I am running out of storage room; but then again, I have orders for 50kg's worth of walnuts, at five euros a kilo.

~

The village *rando*, or walk, is nocturnal, and organized by the Foyer Rural but reliant on the community network, hidden like tree roots; out of sight, but always there, always effective. The course through the woods is marked by the local hunters, the *jambon* which forms the mains of the returnees meal sup-plied by the town butcher, the wine supplied by the village winemakers, the bread baked by a hunter's son.

I do not exaggerate here; the Foyer Rural meeting to discuss the food for the *rando* spent forty-five minutes of discussion on the best cooking method for the *jambon*, and best supplier; at one stage, Jean-François, the president, even phoned a friend for advice.

In a land where the eating of food is taken seriously, there is the expectation that its growing is respected.

Eighty people turn up for the *rando*, a five-kilometre walk which finishes in moonlight in a clearing in the trees, the food taken at trestle tables in marquees. The cost per person was ten euros. The sense of belonging was priceless.

~

Coming down the hill towards the house, a man with a dog and a basket, this full to overflowing with cep mushrooms picked from the woods. The figure is me. For the last week I have joined the cavalcade of villagers, armed with baskets and bags, going into the woods to pick *champignons*. Everybody has their favoured place, and I had to wood-wander through the fallen leaves for an hour till I found my own secret mushroom garden, an enchanted dip ringed with boulders, lost in the middle of five thousand acres of trees: a former sleeping place of wild boar. It was not off the beaten track, it was on it; I was led there by hoof prints dinned into the ground. Overnight rain has caused ceps – the most prized of fungi by chefs, who lexico-graphically upgrade it to 'porcini' – to erupt from the dark earth. (*Boletus edulis* is one of the first autumn fungi, a certain sign of the turning year.) I cut a dozen yesterday, these encouraged into existence by the recent rain, and left a similar number standing, the oblation for Nature. Ceps are beloved by inverte-brates and rodents, as well as gastronomes, real or self-fancied. With its round and sticky top, the cep is fortunately difficult to confuse with other fungi; the English colloquial name of 'sticky bun' captures its appearance perfectly. (Some pharmacies in France, incidentally, will identify mushrooms free of charge, a useful service for the nervous and the novice mushroom-gatherer.) An outstanding mature cep can weigh a kilo and reach 25cm across. One of mine, on the scales at home, weighs in at a creditable 388g.

Cèpes à la Bordelaise

A local Charente recipe given to me by my neighbour, Valérie, who insists that the *cèpes* should not be washed, and smaller *cèpes* are tastier than larger specimens.

800g small, very firm porcini mushrooms
6 sprigs flat-leaf parsley
4 tbsp olive oil

salt and pepper
2 shallots, finely chopped
1 garlic clove, finely chopped
2 tbsp wine (Pineau des Charentes)

Cut off the earthy foot of the mushroom's stalk, and separate the stalk from the head. Cut the stalk into very small cubes, slice the head into 1cm-thick strips.

Rinse the parsley in cool water and pat it dry with paper towels. Remove the large stems and finely chop.

Heat half the oil in a sauté pan over fairly high heat. When it is hot, put in the *cèpes*, season, and simmer for fifteen minutes, shaking the pan several times until the mushrooms are golden brown and the water emitted from the mushrooms has nearly evaporated.

While the mushrooms are simmering, soften the shallots and garlic with the rest of the oil in a small saucepan over low heat. Add the *pineau*. Heat a vegetable dish.

Pour the contents of the saucepan into the sauté pan, mix, cover and cook gently for another minute. Pour into the hot vegetable dish and sprinkle with parsley.

NOVEMBER

Interesting, winter in the Charente. The gauge of winter's start is the going of the lizards. On 'Toussaint', 1 November, the lizards were still scribbling over the gold face of the house, and I was wearing shorts, as I had every day since mid-March. 'Toussaint', a contraction of 'Tous les Saints', meaning 'All Saints', is a public holiday, and the French pay their respects to the dead by placing pots of chrysanthemums on the graves. (French cemeteries, which tend to be stark and stony, suddenly erupt with colour at Toussaint, in the way that deserts bloom with flowers after rain.)

On Armistice Day, another bank holiday – the French take Remembrance seriously – we stood solemnly in the cemetery as Madame la Maire read out the names of the villagers 'Morts pour La France' in the two World Wars, plus the Algerian War. The sky was impossibly blue and the *tricolore* bowed decorously, without movement.

After the service we adjourned to the *salle des fêtes* for the *pot d'amitié,* the friendship drink; in rural France, ritual and rhythm mark the days. Yesterday, entering the agricultural merchants', a chalked board informed me that it was the day of 'Sainte Léone'; every day is a saint's day in France. The free calendar from the bank, which you would have thought was the tribune of Mammon, gives the saint for each of the 365 days of the year. Any attempt at the Foyer Rural to organize an event has to clear Claudine flicking through the calendar on her smartphone: 'But that is Pentecost, that is Ascension . . .' The sacred dates of the French year moor us, tie us together in community, structure life. On that day, 11 November, we walked home, up the stone track from the village, through Guillaume's farmyard, sending the chickens fluttering, a matter of two hundred yards. By the time we reached the house, *les lézards* had disappeared into the crevices of hibernation, vanished as if they had never existed. So too the mosquitoes. By the afternoon of 11 November, I wanted the sanctuary state of hibernation myself. A wind of a million steel knives started up, rattling the shutters.

It was that afternoon that we found, on the lawn of the courtyard, a baby garden dormouse. Despite having fallen thirty feet from the attic where the garden dormice nest, it was alive, and apparently unhurt.

My first close-up meeting with a *lérot* was one summer night when I heard a munching noise on the windowsill of the dining room. I'd put out the remnants of a baguette to bake in the sun – baguette hardened so it cracks like biscuit is the standard French treat for a horse and donkey. Turning on the dining-room light, a ridiculous, cartoon creature looked in through the window at me. *Lérots* are masked, and saved from rodent 'rattiness' by having furred tails. They are also outstanding acrobats; their exit from our attic is along an electricity cable, four floors up. They accomplish it with aplomb. Unless they are babies.

The vet was shut, so we bought a box of Biocanina 'Lait maternisé' ('Fabriqué en France'), with rodents among suitable recipients, from the pharmacy in Chefnay, and fed the *lérot* from a pipette. Snuggled her in torn tissue in a shoebox, placed on a radiator. Of course, she got a name: Létitia. By day three, Létitia and I had a rapport; she would cling to the rear of my thumb to feed. She squeaked with excitement. We bought her a des res Zolux plastic cage, with all the amenities, and wheels. I would get up in the middle of the night to feed her. She commenced on hard food, nibbling an apple. But we ran out of time: dormice hibernate. And to hibernate, they put on weight, lots of it.

We could no longer hear her family scampering around in the attic. Whatever I did could not get enough weight on Létitia. She fought for life every day. But we could not beat the clock.

We buried her, in a tiny grave lined with blue plumbago petals, and the soft toy she liked to snuggle, in the walled front garden, under the flowering cherry trees. Where the family pets go.

~

12 November: looking out of the study window. The lingering leaves on the lime trees are jaundice-hued. The wind whips the leaves on the ground, which flutter up trying to re-find the sky, their position in life. Fighting death. The lack of leaves changes the perspective: we have a clear view down to the *mairie*, and in the early evening gloom spot the lights of cars on the hill across the shallow valley.

The bitter wind vibrates the wires of the mini-vineyard; a screaming lyre. The spindles' berries are fluorescent pink. A hoar frost blackens and softens the remaining walnut leaves, which hang in the tree like stranded kelp from a tide long ago receded. The foxes yap in the wood, clear as tolling bells. Every evening, I shut in the chickens and geese earlier and earlier, and with greater worry.

The lights blow upstairs: Claude the electrician is again down in Cognac for a week. So I fix them myself.

~

I was woken yesterday at 7.04 a.m. by the blackbird 'chinking' at the end of the garden, where it roosts in the lilac. A blackbird in blackness still; in Central European Time November dawn does not occur till nearly 8 a.m.

When I threw open the shutters, the bedroom light caught two green eyes picking their way along the lane; so the cause of the blackbird's alarm was the usual suspect, a cat returning from night-hunting. It's an old disturbance in the French countryside, *chat et merle*.

The Protestant work ethic sits ill with waiting for an 8 a.m. start and sufficient light to see your way. So, for forty-five useless minutes I twiddled my fingers, made *noisettes*, studied the 'To Do' list stuck on the office wall. November in French farming is odd-job month; all the big tasks, the reapings and sowings, of crop and livestock, are done. Yesterday the top of my bitty A4-long 'To Do' list was 'Rotovate *potager* and plant garlic'. Garlic has to get cold to germinate.

Eventually, there was light. The sun birthed out of mist . . . and the Charente did its thing. By 8.30 a.m. the sky was as blue as our shutters, the collared doves on the kitchen roof were cooing gently, and I was wheeling the Jardimeca T180 tiller by its cow-horn handlebars to the *potager*.

After three pulls on the cord the Jardimeca coughed into life, in much the way that fag smokers do. The fire-engine-red Jardimeca is made by Pubert, the French company that claims to be the current 'worldwide leader in tiller manufacture'. Be that as it may, the Jardimeca's sixteen steel blades are borrowed from Boudicca's chariot. The Jardimeca is uncompromising, insatiable even on our stony land.

I had earmarked a flat twenty-yard-by-ten-yard stretch for the garlic. It was virgin land, and the noise of stones hitting the metal guards was a pandemonium. Like a foundry at full speed. Like hail on a cold tin roof. Twenty times or more the Jardimeca hit a clanking boulder, and I needed to stop to prise the offending geology out with a chisel bar. The disinterred boulders were of course added to the edge of the *potager*; the white wall is now almost two feet high, with a fossil in almost every stone; memorials to fallen sea creatures.

Up the escarpment, the Robans are also ploughing. Guillaume's plough hits a boulder; it takes him, his father, his son and me to excavate it; it is the size of a meteorite.

Even with the Jardimeca turned off for these interludes of excavation, there was din. A flock of a hundred starlings was doing its own digging work among the knee-high stalks of the post-harvest sunflower field next door. The starlings whistled and 'wrrrd'; the same sounds as dial-up internet.

⁓

Autumn is a time of closing down, of hibernation. (I have not seen a whip snake or a wall lizard in the garden for a week.) Autumn, though, is also a time of opening up. The leaves of the trees, the limes and the oaks and the planes, were ripped down by a storm rolling in from the Atlantic last week, so as I fought the tiller I possessed long views on the turns. On a low hill to the far west, across the big country, the blades of the wind turbines turned as rhythmically as those of the Jardimeca itself.

As I trudged behind the tiller, I became absorbed by smells: the hot liquorice noisomeness of the Jardimeca's working engine; the mustiness of the churned ochre, white-flecked earth (with after-aroma of bleachy cleanliness). There was something in the air too, something iron and dramatic, though its identity eluded me for a while.

Anyway, after about two hours of tillering, an hour of raking, I was ready to plant the four crates of garlic (a violet, soft-neck variety, Germidour). In Classical cultures, garlic was taken by athletes to improve performance, and administered to toilers to provide health and strength. According to the Greek historian Herodotus, inscriptions on the side of the pyramids recorded that '1,600 talents of silver were spent' on garlic for the slaves, about £20 million at current exchange rates. It did occur to me, as I took out the first bulb from the wooden crate, that I could do with a taste of my own medicine; or rather, my knee could. And it was as I planted that first bulb I realized what the elusive smell in the air was: winter.

~

My peasant, self-sufficient life: I am working no fewer hours than I did when I was farming commercially (still the twelve-hour day), but the ethos is the relaxing difference. The baseline is no longer 'What can we sell, for how much' to the middle man, but 'Are we providing for ourselves?' In Britain, if one was a self-declared self-sufficient, eyebrows would be raised, smirks gather at the corners of mouths, and pigeonholes of naivety apportioned. In France, the attitude is a remark-less, 'Bien sûr.' Today, I joined the Confédération Paysanne, the national trade union for peasants. I am, frankly, unable to resist its manifesto, and its history – which includes ploughing up the Champs de Mars, the park at the foot of the Eiffel Tower, in protest against unsustainable farming – and its aim for 'more autonomous, more relocated systems with the objective of providing healthy, quality and diversified food to all'.

On the way out of the house, I caught sight of a dark-tanned man I did recognize. It was me, caught in the hall mirror. I live outdoors, not just at work, but in my free time, of meals, relaxation, reading.

Penny and the dogs, all three of them now, come down the track as I am bashing the sunflower heads, to separate the seeds into a bin. No art is required. Up in the woods, the wild sounds of *la chasse* starting up. 'It is odd,' says Penny. 'I seem to have become used to the sound of gunfire.'

Ah, autumn in France *profonde*. The glint of sun on gathered grapes, the spicy perfume of the sunflower harvest, the wild cry of hounds as *la chasse* courses through the misty forest.

The hunting season in France, which begins as early as August in some north-eastern departments, is in full swing. Inevitably, there will be deaths between now and March, when the season closes. According to the National Office of Hunting and Wildlife (ONCFS), since 1999 more than 3,000 shooting accidents have occurred, with in excess of 420 mortalities. Some of the dead were absolute innocents: a sixty-nine-year-old woman was shot in her own garden after a hunter fired through her hedge; a driver was killed by a bullet that had rebounded off a wild boar. Most of the dead, however, are hunters themselves. The ONCFS attributes the mortalities of French hunting to 'a failure to comply with basic safety rules'. In exegesis, one needs to acknowledge the nature of the game in the Hexagon: significant beasts on the French 'to-shoot list' are deer and wild boar, both of which require a round from a rifle – which can spin a projectile a kilometre – as opposed to the shotgun, which is standard in British shooting, the range of which is mere metres. Yet the most obvious, and the most culturally significant, reason for the mortalities of French hunting is the sheer number of people involved in the pursuit. If the number of registered hunters has gone down since the start of the century, it still stands at 1.2 million. By a longshot, hunting is France's third most popular hobby, after rugby and football.

Hunting in France is part of the national bloodstream, part of France's sense of itself. France is stubbornly rural; in a detailed portrait of France, published in July, Insee, the national statistics office, determined that the rural areas of France hold 88 per cent of all local councils and 33 per cent of the population. (The European average is 28 per cent.) However, France's rural population inhabits 551,500 km^2, making the mainland population density eleven persons per km^2, or about a quarter that of England. Thus, Insee concluded, France is the second most rural country in Europe after Poland.

In France, unlike in the UK, hunting is not primarily an elite activity; *les chasseurs* in our neck of the Charente woods are the local butcher, the *boulanger*, the garage mechanic, the nurse and the peasant farmer, who all tip up in white Citroën Berlingo vans. Us, and definitely not Them.

Quite literally, hunting in France is not up on its high horse; the local hunters primarily hunt on foot, rather than aboard an equine. The right to shoot game was won from the aristocracy during the Revolution, and if French property rights are abstruse, it is generally accepted, courtesy of 1789 and All That, that hunters have a right to roam, unless formally forbidden by the land owner. In France, hunting is a revolutionary act, as opposed to confirmation of class status.

Why do *les chasseurs* go out on a Sunday with a gun? Some are pragmatic. 'It is food on the table, and will keep the family going for a week,' one acquaintance told me about the wild boar in the back of the van. (Never underestimate rural poverty; the cities always get the money, and if you doubt it, try getting a bus in rural France. They do not exist, so we live by the car.) For others the hunt, in killing the crop-destroying boar and deer, is performing its public duty. Many seek immersion in Nature, and a finding of their inner selves. Or, as Spaniard José Ortega y Gasset described in *Meditations on Hunting*, 'One does not hunt in order to kill; on the contrary, one kills in order to have hunted.'

Voices are continuously raised against hunting, petitions delivered to the Élysée. The hunters respond by demonstrating on the streets. Well, France is the country of Asterix.

There has been hunting in France since the Paleolithic people painted animal scenes on the walls of the caves at Lascaux in the Dordogne. Hunting will take some killing, and the French countryside will continue to be speckled with little metal signs in the *tricolore*'s red, white and blue announcing land to be a 'Réserve de Chasse et de Faune Sauvage' under a government directive from 1991. But you would be mad to walk near a French wood while 'la chasse est en cours'.

～

When we drive west from the house to the beach (just an hour away, to the delight of my family, used to landlocked Herefordshire), we cross the Chemin Saint-Jacques, the pilgrimage route to Santiago de Compostela in Spain, marked by a stylized scallop shell. Reputedly, the remains of St James the Apostle are buried in the city. The Way of Saint James became a major pilgrimage route of medieval Christianity, but its popularity dwindled during the Wars of Religion; it was revived in 1957 with *The Road to Santiago*, a travelogue by the Irish Hispanist Walter Starkie. In the 1980s the route was declared the first European Cultural Route by the Council of Europe.

Anyway, one day, as we crossed the signal brass scallops set among the stones of Saint-Jeán-d'Angély's main square, Tris asked me, 'Couldn't we do a section of the walk?' And so a month later, after getting ourselves kitted out at the Decathlon store in Niort, Tris and I arrived at Saint-Jean-Pied-de-Port, a small town sitting pretty at the French base of the Pyrenees. With its white chalet-style houses, precision-stacked cords of wood under long eaves, it is typical of mountain towns in Continental Europe.

Less usually, Saint-Jean has a passport office. At number 39, on the cobbled rue de la Citadelle, those undertaking the historic Camino Francés pilgrimage from France to Santiago de Compostela in Spain collect their *carnet de pèlerin*.

The staff of the passport office keep late hours. Tris and I arrived at nearly eight in the evening, after time lost down sequentially slower SNCF rail track; the woman on duty was unfailingly helpful, did the paperwork, talked us through the path, which is acknowledged to be difficult. Day One is a six-hour climb of a thousand metres, followed by an hour or so of ragged, shaley descent.

In total, twenty-six kilometres distance. As the raven flies.

And the weather can turn. People die doing the Camino. The Hollywood actor Martin Sheen starred in a film 'inspired' – no, not the *mot juste*; I should write 'prompted' – by such a tragedy, *The Way*, released in 2010.

The passport official's parting advice as we left for our *pension* was: 'Do not start too early. In the dark, you might get lost.'

Dutifully, we emerged at daybreak next morning, but into mist as thick as shroud. A conundrum: if we started much later we might not get over the mountains in daylight. We decided to go, hoisted our 15kg packs on our back. (I call such luggage a 'haversack'; Tris laughs and says, 'Just pack'; I wear 'old school' pink shorts for such Outward Bound stuff, he has Lycra-type 'breathable' trousers. Such are the generational differences.)

For a kilometre or more, I saw nothing other than white mist – some of it of my own making: my breath – and tarmac, and stone. I was parallel to a cliff.

The climb out of town was a mere *amuse-bouche*. A teaser. Mauve crocuses on the wayside consoled. Then our heads were out of the bag of fog. At the top of the lane, framed by bare chestnut trees, was the view: saw-toothed mountains opening up the blue belly of the sky.

Sunshine blared on frozen peaks.

Surely, I thought, we are not going over those?

Surely, we were.

A climb up a mountain is an ascension through climatic and ecological layers. The little alpine meadows were left behind; then we lost the trees, save on western slopes, where the holm oaks lay in grey cloud banks.

We reached the high grassland. Tundra. Rocks the size of buffalo grazed.

For a mad moment, I heard chimes on the wind, then realized it was no delirium. Charolais cows, seemingly glued to the slopes, wore tonkling bells around their necks. So did the sheep. So did the lovely brown, blond-maned ponies.

All the animals had brass bells on. Melodic tinnitus.

On the long open stretches, we could see, in front and behind, fellow pilgrims penguin-shuffling: the steepness retarded speed.

On a concrete cistern beside the path, sprayed in bright black paint, was the enjoinment 'Keep Going'.

Historically, the Pilgrimage to Santiago enjoyed its peak of popularity between the eleventh and sixteenth centuries. Recent decades, though, have seen a resurgence in numbers. About 200,000 people a year take the Way, mostly Spanish Catholics. But pilgrims come in all types. Each has a tale to tell, a revelation to hope for.

Me? I am of the George Mallory school. When asked about Everest, the mountaineer retorted, 'Because it is there.'

So for me, Mallory and God. I believe I am the last religious nature writer.

Also, you can take the boy off the farm, you cannot take the farm out of the boy; my agriculturalist's eye noted the incontrovertible truth as we proceeded to the Heavens; in the city the rich live on the heights, in the country 'tis the poor.

We passed a stubble-cheeked sheep farmer plugging a gap in his wire fence with a wooden pallet. In response to our 'Bonjour' he lifted the index finger of his right hand – a salutary essay in the economy of effort.

Above him, the electricity cables were strung to their rightful post with pink bailer twine.

We went up, always up. Behind us, the cars and the white farmhouses miniaturized; it was the vertical view out of an aircraft window.

The weather was good to us, clear and blue.

Up, always up. We passed fellow pilgrims, wishing them, as they wished us, 'Bon Camino.'

Vultures joined the pilgrimage. Five Egyptian vultures. Spiralling around on horizontal sails of wings.

A party of red kites tagged on behind the vultures; an aerial caravanserai to match our pilgrims' progress.

Scavengers, those birds, the lot of them; birds who do no killing of their own. In the Pyrenees the precipices and the weather do their murder for them.

On a path pounded into the rock by countless feet in forgotten eras, we crossed the Spanish border. Every fifty metres a wooden post announced the emergency phone number, 113. A vulture, perched on a cascade of scree, brazenly eyed us up.

. . . And then was no more up: there was only below. We had summited, reached the absolute, snowy top of the 1,410-metre Collado Lepoeder. Far beneath our feet, solid and secure amid the serene beeches of the Iraty Forest, was the monastery of Roncesvalles.

The monastery is the pilgrims' hostel for the night. Pleasure on achieving its thick walls on this hardest of days, on this best of days, was sobered by the marker indicating the path to be taken the next morning: Santiago de Compostela 790km.

Below, some pilgrim, some time, had scribbled on the sign with a big felt pen marker, 'Walk. Don't reach.'

It's the journey, stupid.

~

23 November. 6.02 p.m. Go out to shut in the fowl. Sun a band of watery blood in the west. Barely light enough to see. Tired by the work, the planting-up additional garlic down in the field by the stream, and life reduced to peremptory phrases. Life in staccato. Then: a red comet across the Robans' wheat field, a hundred metres from the house. (We are, of course, hedgeless in our neighbourly demarcation; stones suffice in the

wide-open land.) At first I believed the horizontal fire-streak a deer, it was so very large; then I recognized the gait.

Fox.

Dog fox burning bright in its winter coat.

Same day: 10 p.m.-ish. Outside a fox barks. Very close by. From the kitchen window, I shine a million-candle-power torch out at the chickens' paddock; a pair of green eyes stare back at me. It's like being under siege. The fox only has to be lucky once. I have to be vigilant always.

The country is the country. Whether Britain or France.

~

In a fit of enthusiasm for home-made cooking oil, I have bought an automatic cold press machine, two hundred euros from the local garden centre. The machine is set up in the *cave*; I funnel in the seeds, press the button … and the sunflower oil comes out. The machine will do walnuts too. We have ten olives on our olive tree in the courtyard. So, maybe, one day olive oil too. The waste, the crushed sunflower seeds, goes to the chickens and geese.

~

Nobody has come for White Dog. So today, 29 November, we officially adopt her, passport her at the vet's, apply for her ID card. Freda, the dog's new, official owner, christens her Honey. Beautifully, and unbeknownst to Freda, my very first dog, when I was seven, was called Honey. And was a golden Labrador.

~

Not a bird sang in a thousand acres. Not even a robin, peeping its imperial claims. I wanted to shout, to shatter the wide monotony of it all.

It was late, and as I trudged through that sort of fine mist one gets with drizzle, the world became more monotone still. Greyscale.

And silent.

In a muddy rut, marks of fox feet, the rear pads fitting exactly into the fore; the prints of a fox – running scared, or running to pounce, one or the other. Briefly I looked for an answer – evidential proof, in the form of feather or fur – but could see nothing. The murk was too great. I, the jury, remained out.

At the fork in the path, I did not haver. I took the path most travelled. The dog had had her exercise. My face was tight with the cold, despite being hunched, tortoise-style, down into the collar of my coat. I wanted to get home, to the fire, the fire made with kindling gathered from this very woodland. A winter wood is a contradiction: the living trees are wire-sharp. Alienating. Hard. But their dead bits provide comfort and warmth. And the pleasure of *cèpes* and oyster mushrooms.

My foot caught against a fallen oak branchlet, long and thin. I bent down and in the gloom picked it up for future use in the hearth: a picture-echo down the ages of Stone Age man.

We were almost out of the woods, the dog and I, when I felt her shrink against my leg. Some snorting about in the undergrowth I had presumed belonged to her clearly did not.

There came fast breathing, some of it mine, in excitement. (Or perhaps, nerves.) Every synapse tuned, electric and keen. I did not move. I was as rooted as the rain-blacked oaks.

A shadow crossed the path ten yards ahead of us, went into the trees, and evanesced.

More than any other European animal, wild boar belong to another age. Prehistory. The time of sabretooth tigers and mammoths. Curiously, I found myself clutching my heavy oak branch and wanting belatedly to hurl it, spear-like, at the boar. To bring home to the cave the bacon.

~

That evening we were invited to dinner by the Martineaus, acquaintances who live at the bottom of the village. The obvious dilemma was what to take as gift, since it would be a foolish English person to take wine to a French meal. In the end we settled for a bottle of port, which we could at least pass off as traditionally English, and half a dozen eggs. Our host Jean-Pierre, a retired pharmacist, looked queryingly at the port, which was consigned to a cupboard, and poured us small glasses of bright blue Benedictine, a liquor whose existence I had forgotten, from a drinks table. As well as Jean-Pierre and his wife, Madeleine, the other guests were Thomas and Elizabeth, who both worked in administration at the local hospital.

It turned out that roast *sanglier* was the main dish, and it came with a tale. Jean-Pierre had bought a whole boar from the local hunt, intending to keep a haunch for himself (the night's meal), the rest going to his copious in-laws. He and Madeleine had popped around to the head of the local hunt yesterday to collect the beast, failing to realize they were buying a frozen boar. This they had transported home, in a mini-trailer behind the car, with the boar's four legs sticking vertically in the air; to avoid distressing fellow motorists they tied a plastic sheet over the corpse. This blew off, as they were being overtaken by an MPV full of children, whose screams at the revealed monster were audible above the engine. After much sweat Jean-Pierre and Madeleine finally managed to get the boar upstairs, into the bath, where it had taken thirty hours to defrost.

As a dinner topic it was, shall we say, an ice-breaker.

Conversation at a French dinner is a minefield, because there are forbidden topics: work, religion and politics are all off the table. It is a way of maintaining peace and quiet, among neighbours and friends. During four hours of chat the closest we got to politics was to wonder whether euthanasia in Switzerland was worth the cost when you could get Jean-Claude, the alcoholic shepherd, to do the job for a hundred euros. Tops. After dessert, I was no wiser about the political views of the gathered diners than I had been when we chatted over the *apéros*.

The French are very good at privacy. Hence their distance-keeping device of the formal *vous* in speech, and the reluctance to use Christian names on first social encounter; these are shutters, as effective as the shutters outside the houses. You can appreciate why; after the Catholic v Protestant Wars of Religion, after the Revolution, and the Resistance/Collaboration of the Second World War, there lingers in France the feeling that you need to be careful what you say, in revealing who you are. So, unlike Britain, you rarely, if ever, see political posters in windows or gardens.

The safe topics for mealtime chat are the production of artisan goat's cheese, rugby (of course), the weather – it's always biblical flood or drought in south-west France – and the career of Nadal, who, despite being born south of the Pyrenees, has effectively been adopted by *les Français*. The peccadilloes of the British or Monégasque royal families never fail as talk-fodder. And then there is the hapless village local who has contravened planning rules; the biggest scandal in the village this whole year has been the newcomer who painted his shutters purple, instead of the regulation blue.

It is a very quiet village. In a very quiet land.

WINTER

DECEMBER

Winter's exposure, winter's erasure; the wind, having defoliated the oak down the track, has revealed the crow's nest, the squirrel's drey. The shutters of the house bang constantly in the wind. From the bottom of the village, the sparky Christmas lights cascade down the tower of the *église*.

Morning: in the paddock the cockerel crows, and the geese released from their hut flay their wings, and for a moment they are airborne, but the wildness goes and then they allow me to herd them out on to the Robans' sunflower stubble fifty metres up the track, so they can glean free grains and forage the array of weed (aka wildflower) seeds. Good for goose health, good too for the taste of goose on the tongue; bland meat comes from bland feeding. In return for the forage, the Robans receive from me a bottle of my home-made *épinette*, and get their land manured.

Such old-fashioned goose-herding comes with its dangers. On the lane earlier in the week, I was hailed down by a neighbour who stuck his head through the car window to say, 'You got some geese on your stubble! Can I shoot them?' I explained, to his disappointment, that said geese are domestic Toulouse, not wild greylag.

Our geese are subject of local talk. Will they be belatedly stuffed for *foie gras*? Will they go to the Christmas lunch table?

People walking around the village stop, stare and practically salivate.

The indispensable phrase in French life is 'C'est compliqué.' Christmas is coming, and the geese are getting fat, and I am rather tempted to put one at least on the table; they are meant to be egg-layers, and not an egg in sight.

Our chickens, meanwhile, continue to lay prodigiously; finally the penny has dropped. Egg-laying in chickens is partly determined by the amount of daylight; there is an hour's more daylight per day here in south-west France than Hereford-shire. So, with my surplus of eggs, I commence a weekly egg round in the village. But every time I drop off a box (two euros) to a neighbour they ask, 'And the geese, will you be selling them for Christmas?'

~

Today, I started French lessons with a human, as opposed to the Hugo cassettes. The Hugo course was excellent, but I allowed language learning to be pushed down my workaday agenda, and somehow never found the time to progress past week eight of the three-month syllabus. Also, my edition was twenty years out of date. I mean it omitted the French habit of abbreviation where adolescents are *ados*, and Verlan's ingress into the language was unforeseen. Verlan is the inversion of syllables in a word to make slang, a slang no longer confined to said *ados* but sufficiently commonplace to be entered into *Petit Larousse*. My French teacher, Nathalie, is a retired translator. She does not take English prisoners, and the hour's lesson is entirely in French. Afterwards, I flake out with my head on the table, and can barely stay awake. The mental effort is exhaust-ing. She has also given me homework, and insisted that I order

Bescherelle's *La conjugaison*. I am conjugating French verbs, I am back at school.

Nathalie is dynamic and brilliant. In Verlan, she is *ouf* (*fou*, with syllables inverted, but with an additional twist in meaning of mad to madly wonderful). I feel almost French. One day I may even be able to pronounce properly '*fauteuil*', French for armchair, which involves tongue and lip movements so eccentric that Mister Bean would struggle.

~

Every Christmas we dress up our donkey, Snowdrop. We paint her hooves glittery silver, put a plaid rug on her back, twiddle some gold tinsel in her head collar. Generally, we make her look Christmassy; she is a village fixture and visited by kids and adults alike. (She loves the attention, and the fuss by the villagers has done something to ameliorate her sadness at Zeb's death. Besides, she has been adopted by the sheep as one of them, or vice versa.) So, I went out this afternoon to do her Noël nail polish, and, en route and on a whim, decided to check the geese in the sunflower stubble. In the back of their mobile shelter, in the straw, an egg. Sure, I would have liked a goose to lay a golden egg, but I will settle for a bright white one.

Next day: two white eggs, and a customer in Claudine, 'la reine de la cuisine' of the village, who avows that goose eggs produce the best gateau. Any temptation to put the geese on the plate is abolished. Our geese will escape Christmas.

There is no shortage of food for Noël, however. I have bartered herbs, fig chutney, pickled eggs, goose eggs, walnuts with some local *bio* producers, young couples starting up, so we have cheese and beef. Every fruit and vegetable need is supplied by fresh or preserved goods from the *potager*. Also, we went to

Britain last weekend, in the Citroën Berlingo, loaded to the gunwales. Customs at Caen were perplexed by the hops, but on discovering that we had nothing illicit hidden under the packets of marjoram, bay, twenty different herbs, jars of pickled walnuts, etc., waved us through. We came back with a lighter van, but heavier wallets, and bought organic salmon from Biocoop in Saint-Jean-d'Angély.

A typical French Christmas *réveillon*, the meal eaten on Christmas Eve after church, can extend to twelve courses. We have managed a reasonable six. Tonight our menu is:

Egg mayonnaise (with sunflower oil)
Salmon tartare
Roast beef/walnut roast (with carrots, green
beans, asparagus, potatoes)
Green salad
Bûche de Noël (a log-shaped chocolate cake)
with blackberry sauce and cream
Cheese and water biscuits with fig chutney
Sloe liqueur chocolates

Drinks: apple juice, *épinette*, *vin de noix*, *vin de maison* (our first bottle; quite 'invigorating' but, as Madame Roban would say, 'At least we know what is in it'), and lastly *pineau*, a gift from our friend Stéphane. The only items bought from a shop were the cream, the water biscuits, the salmon and the *bûche de Noël*.

That night: up here on a faraway hill, I do my last round of animal-checking and bedding down. The air is cold, the million stars are close. I break open a bale of hay for the sheep. It is a silent night, and the peace of the tended farm animals is at once restful and profound; below sleeps under starlight the little French village of La Roche. It is a real-life Christmas card.

~

Boxing Day. This morning we all walked up to the woods with the dogs, and all came back carrying some foraged branches; such scavenging of wood is now instinctual.

I write this from the sitting room, with the sofa pushed back to make space for our now three dogs, blissed out in front of the fire. When the rescue dog Honey is not conked on the Persian rug, she sits and looks at the Christmas tree, with its lights and baubles. Her present was a rubber bone with a ball inside; she loves to play with toys. A second youth. 'Hi, Honey,' we say to her every day, 'you are now home.' I know the feeling.

~

In the twilight, I have just planted, in the hedge we are encouraging along the track, a spindle tree, a cherry and a fig. A kestrel, flame-tipped in the dying sun, sat on the telephone wire and kept me company. After admiring my handiwork, I have come in to do something I am apprehensive of: a tally sheet of my autarky endeavour. It takes a while, and a borrowed calculator, but, when I factor in bartering and goods sold, we achieved 50 per cent food self-sufficiency by autumn. And it was ours, and it was good. 'Bon goût,' exclaimed Jean-Luc, a self-confessed gastronome, kissing his lips with his fingers in comment on our bartered goose eggs. Sure, to achieve this 50 per cent we threw away nothing, not a peel, a stalk, a core. But is that a bad thing? Modern households throw away 30 per cent of food purchased. We wasted nothing. *Rien.*

True, we still have not made *pineau*, but what is life without missed targets, and something still to aim for? Anyway, perhaps such tick-list surveys miss the point. In my self-sufficiency, I was self-fulfilled; and the earth, the plants, and the animals – the wild and the domestic – and I were one. Indivisible.

This morning, a red deer doe was nibbling the briars in the orchard hedge, briars being a standard iron ration for the species. I was at the hedge, collecting berries and green foliage for the family to weave around the wooden spiral staircase as Christmas decoration. The berries of rowan, spindle, hawthorn and rosehip were brilliant red, Christ-blood scarlet. Seasonal. The sky was impossibly blue, and the quiet lay like a goose-feather quilt on the land. But the cold flailed in thousands of small razors.

My head wanted the deer on a plate, my heart ached at its innocent beauty, the lustrous red of its coat.

~

I love Paris in the wintertime. The city is suited best by December's soft, cloudy grey: perfect for musing in cafés, for romance, for the idle pleasure of walking wet cobbled backstreets, a *bar-tabac* on the corner, a story behind the wrought-iron doorway of every apartment block.

When we arrived in Paris yesterday, up on the high-speed TGV from Angoulême, there was still mist on the Seine. The *vedettes*, the tourist boats, had not yet started plying their trade, but a barge forced its way upstream through water the colour of lead. In the hold was heaped gravel, though the real cargo of a Seine barge is sadness. Incongruously, the name of the barge was 'Summer'. Her ensign was wrapped around the flagpole, limp as a wet rag.

In the flower market, the vendors were arranging fluorescent tulip bouquets under the dripping nineteenth-century iron-and-glass roof.

A *bouquiniste*, scarf knotted around his neck, arrived on the quayside by Mobylette to open his green book-box. The first titles out were on the philosopher Jacques Lacan and the actor Jean-Paul Belmondo.

Paris est toujours Paris.

We were in Paris for the same reason as everyone else: to fill our heads with culture, to fill our bags with couture.

It seems an absurdist irony that the most alluring of museums for the Nature lover is situated in the most urban of places. The Musée de la Chasse et de la Nature has inhabited the seventeenth-century Hôtel de Guénégaud at 62 rue des Archives, Paris, since 1967, and from 2007 incorporated the next door, and equally elegant, Hôtel de Mongelas. Then one remembers that Paris is the city of the intellect, and the *musée* has always possessed philosophical and artistic aspirations. Congenitally, as proclaimed by its title, the museum celebrates the history of hunting and, by conceptual extension, the human meeting with the natural world. The museum – which, in a quintessentially French republican fudge, is private but open to the public, at ten euros a ticket – is laid out like a shooting aesthete's luxurious mansion, mixing antique hunting weapons (an entire room), trophies, paintings by masters, wooden cabinets with animal curios (bleached skulls) and large taxidermy creatures, notably a brown bear on its hind legs, which neither adult nor child can resist for a smartphone 'selfie'. Then some object placed provocatively disrupts nostalgia and platitude; I have walked the rooms of the *musée* over the last decade or so to encounter a ceramic Scottie by pop artist Jeff Koons in the

Salon of the Dogs, or an animatronic albino boar head, not to forget the alcove of unicorns. It is the thinking countryperson's museum.

After the Musée de la Chasse et de la Nature, came post-Christmas shopping in the bright boutiques of the Marais district, once a *pauvre*, ghettoey, stinking marsh, now come-up chic. Quai 71 and Kenzo got the best of the children's Xmas money. Penny and I sat out the shopping on a nearby brasserie terrace, watching the world go by over a *noisette* and a *grand crème*. As you do, in Paris. As you do in France.

Naturally, after the post-Christmas shopping we took the antidote. Paris might be poor in the number of its green spaces (the city has just 8.8 per cent canopy cover, whereas Oslo has 28.8 per cent), but the Jardin des Tuileries in the 1st arrondissement is my favourite park on the planet. It is also a site of family mythology. Penny and I came here with the children on our first ever family trip abroad. At the stone ponds – raised, two feet above ground – the toy-yacht stand was closed for winter. (There is a perfect, immortal painting of the ponds with wooden *petits bateaux* under sail, Picasso's post-Impressionist *Le Bassin des Tuileries*, from 1901.) Yesterday, in the stead of small boats on carefree journeys, black-headed gulls drifted aimlessly to music from two bored teenagers with a beat box.

We sat on the green iron chairs, and watched the birds go by. A raven shuffled about, cocked its black head aside, and peered into my eyes. My raven took his chance to people-watch, reverse the order of things.

Our Paris rituals tend to end with dinner at La Coupole, the most famous of the old Parisian brasseries. The Art Deco restaurant is vast, under (as the name indicates) a huge dome, the entire edifice kept upright by pillars ornately painted by leading artists of the Roaring Twenties, notably Henri Matisse and Fernand Léger. La Coupole was where the intellectual great and the good used to go. Sartre. Papa Hem. Camus. De Beauvoir. Yesterday, while we ate in golden, lambent light, the conversation of the room rose in a warm, polyphonic tide. La Coupole: a profane temple of talk.

Time passed. Too fast. The meal became another Bateman cartoon: 'The customers who said "Non" to liqueurs at La Coupole.' Our perfectly attentive waiter was aghast at our refusal.

We explained we had a train to catch.

'Ah, le train,' he replied, with an exasperated throw of arms and a 'Pfffff'. The immutability of the SNCF timetable. What can you do?

As our train pulled out of Gare Montparnasse on time to the second, rain lashed the coaches, and I thought of the wild boar at home in the Charente night, coming out of the forest into the wheat field. Then came into my mind: the cry of the stone curlews echoing off the chalk escarpment, and the 'kerwicking' of the tawny in the lime trees in front of the house, planted by a priest a century ago. My mind also pictured my *potager*, the sheep, the geese, the chickens, Snowdrop the donkey, the orchards, the three paddocks. And a hayloft full of food, raised by my own hands.

J'aime Paris. Yet, I still wanted the train to go faster.

The birds of La Roche (as seen in the garden and the two paddocks adjacent to the house)

Great tit, swallow, starling, robin, collared dove (nesting), redstart (nesting), black redstart (nesting), little owl, blackcap, spotted flycatcher, jay, red-legged partridge, greenfinch, long-tailed tit, goshawk, house sparrow, stone curlew, wood pigeon (nesting), goldfinch, house martin, wren (nesting), blackbird (nesting), pied wagtail, black kite, hoopoe, swallow (nesting), song thrush, turtle dove, cirl bunting, swift, greater spotted woodpecker, ortolan bunting, chaffinch, chiffchaff, kestrel, pheasant, firecrest, hen harrier, nightjar, fieldfare, whitethroat, garden warbler, peregrine falcon, linnet, cattle egret (overhead), hawfinch.

La Vie, *a playlist: the essential classics*

Juliette Armanet, 'Le dernier jour du disco'
Charles Aznavour, 'Emmenez-moi'
Brigitte Bardot, 'Harley Davidson'
Alain Bashung, 'Osez Joséphine'
Amel Bent, 'Ma philosophie'
Gilbert Bécaud, 'Et maintenant'
Jacques Brel, 'Ne me quitte pas'
Christophe, 'Les Mots bleus'
Francis Cabrel, 'La Corrida'
Dalida with Alain Delon, 'Paroles, paroles'
Joe Dassin, 'Les Champs-Élysées'
Eddy de Pretto, 'Kid'
Claude François, 'Comme d'habitude'
France Gall, 'Résiste'
Serge Gainsbourg and Jane Birkin, 'Je t'aime . . . moi non plus'
Jean-Jacques Goldman, 'Quand la musique est bonne'
Johnny Hallyday, 'Allumer le feu'
Françoise Hardy, 'Tous les garçons et les filles'
Indochine, 'L'Aventurier'
Philippe Katerine, 'Louxor, j'adore'
Clara Luciani, 'La Grenade'
Vanessa Paradis, 'Joe le taxi'
Edith Piaf, 'La Vie en rose'
Plastic Bertrand, 'Ça plane pour moi'
Les Rita Mitsouko, 'C'est comme ça'
Véronique Sanson, 'Amoureuse'
Stromae, 'Formidable'
Téléphone, 'Cendrillon'
Charles Trenet, 'La Mer'

John Lewis-Stempel is a farmer and 'Britain's finest living nature writer' (*The Times*). His books include the *Sunday Times* bestsellers *Woodston*, *The Running Hare* and *The Wood*. He is the only person to have won the Wainwright Prize for Nature Writing twice, with *Meadowland* and *Where Poppies Blow*. In 2016 he was named Magazine Columnist of the Year for his column in *Country Life*. He farms cattle, sheep, pigs and poultry. (Traditionally.)